Praise

"It's compassionate, formative...A game-changer that does more than explain trauma; it offers a compassionate roadmap to healing. With practical tools, profound insights, and a rare level of raw honesty in self-help literature, this book transformed my understanding of my own experiences."

—**TOM DEWOLF,** author of *The Little Book of Racial Healing and Inheriting the Trade*

"Collins offers a deeply insightful and transformative exploration of trauma and the pathways to healing. With a compassionate voice and a wealth of practical tools, Collins equips readers with the necessary resources to identify the lingering effects of past pain and gently guides them toward breaking free from limiting patterns."

—**ALKEMIA EARTH,** Founder and CEO of the Ascension Academy and Certified Master Energy Medicine Practitioner

"This book, filled with personal insights and practical strategies, provides hope and a tangible toolkit for black veterans and individuals of all backgrounds to mend their emotional and mental scars, emerging stronger and more resilient. Dr. Collins' approach, which blends science with spirituality, offers a practical and holistic path to recovery."

—**CHAD BROWN,** Founder of Soul River Inc. and Love is King, conservationist, film director, and photographer

"Dr. Collins has laid out a comprehensive guide to trauma and healing trauma that will benefit just about everyone. She lays out what trauma is beautifully and provides many tools for regulating the nervous system and returning to wholeness."

—DR. CHARMAYNE KILCUP-KLUNA, author of *Heal Your Heart*

"A masterful roadmap for healing—offering profound insights and practical tools that are not just theoretical but can be applied in real life to break destructive cycles, rebuild resilience, and rediscover joy. With compassion and expertise, Collins transforms trauma recovery from an overwhelming challenge into an achievable, empowering journey."

—DAWN EIDELMAN, PHD, Executive Director, Association for Comprehensive Energy Psychology, executive coach, and award-winning education entrepreneur

"Collins' deeply compassionate approach and insightful three-level framework resonate, mirroring the ancient Hawaiian practice of Ho'oponopono. Her personal narrative and coaching stories provide a relatable and safe space for readers to confront their trauma while offering practical tools."

—KUMU RAMSAY TAUM, Director at the Pacific Island Leadership Institute (PILI) at Hawaii Pacific University, Founder and Kumu in Residence at the Life Enhancement Institute of the Pacific in Hawai'i

"Drawing from her personal experiences, expertise as an educator, and knowledge of interpersonal neurobiology, Collins creates an accessible and practical resource that empowers those seeking healing and resilience. The book offers a clear and structured approach."

—MARY ANDRUS DAT, LCAT, LPC, ATCS, Assistant Professor and Co-Director Lewis and Clark Graduate College Arts In Healing International Film Festival Art Therapy Graduate Program

"As a reader traveling her own path of healing from trauma, I felt lovingly held by Dr. Collins' words. An accessible overview of the science of trauma and the trauma response paired with an abundant toolkit of practices, this book offers a powerful guide in the healing process."

—**MATSYA SIOSAL,** writer, facilitator, and Director for the Center for Community Engagement Lewis & Clark Graduate School of Education and Counseling

"Collins has created a roadmap to healing that speaks directly to women whose lives have been shaped by unaddressed trauma. With remarkable clarity and compassion, she transforms complex concepts into actionable insights."

—**NIKKI WEAVER,** artist, yoga teacher, and Director of On The Inside Art-Based Education for Incarcerated Women

"Collins shares her profound wisdom and insights forged from a lifetime of emotional labor and extensive scientific research. It is both an intellectual and experiential road map to awareness and healing. The exercises and journaling deepen the reader's consciousness while strengthening new habits."

—**PHIL JOHNSON,** Founder and CEO, Master of Business Leadership Program

"Collins bridges the gap between trauma scholarship and personal experience, offering scientific foundations, and practical wisdom. Through plain-spoken guidance and carefully woven personal narratives, she provides a roadmap for healing from abuse, neglect, addiction, racism, and other identity-based harms."

—**KATIE MANSFIELD, PHD,** STAR (Strategies for Trauma Awareness and Resilience) Trainer, Facilitator of arts-based, embodied learning and Founder of Rekindling LLC

"A heartfelt soul journey fearlessly written by a professional woman of color who can convey the challenging and often painful, wrenching patterns and hurtful experiences of trauma. Shared in a touching, poignant manner, she has compiled a book chock-full of useful, easy energy techniques and practical advice."

—REV. DR. ADARA L. WALTON, ND, PHD, author of *Every Body's Truth*

THE

TRUTH

ABOUT

TRAUMA

About the Author

Lisa Y. Collins is a respected trauma healing leader, life coach, trauma practitioner, author, and assistant professor. Her studies focus on healing through a personal analysis of trauma.

© Nina Johnson Photography

Lisa's consulting includes nonprofit and for-profit organizations, including local educational systems, the Association for Comprehensive Energy Psychology, the Shift Network, and the Center for Justice and Peace Building. She utilizes her skills to provide healing within organizations and individuals.

Her first book, *Love of Light: A Guide to Peace and Oneness*, guides consciousness, boosts self-awareness, and provides tools for living in peace. Her past podcast, *Love and Light Living Every Day in Peace*, focused on positive examples of healing practices in the world.

As a playwright, she has had works produced in New York and Portland, and her acclaimed short film, *Be Careful What You Ask For*, serves as a platform for racial healing discussions and has won an award in Make Art Not Fear and was accepted into Manhattan Rep's STORIES Film Festival and Portland Film Festival. Her engaging TEDx Talk, "Healing from Racial Trauma," also chronicles the healing modalities that resulted for herself and others from her research.

Lisa uses her spiritual gifts as an intuitive, spiritual writer, and playwright to provide healing and openness that acknowledges humankind's intersectionality. In addition, she uses her life coach and spirituality skills to give acceptance and space for connectedness and oneness in a world that needs it so much.

Lisa lives in Portland, Oregon, with her wife, the youngest of her four children, and their cat, Hunter.

THE

TRUTH

ABOUT

TRAUMA

Break
Patterns

Build
Resilience

Restore
Joy

Lisa Collins EdD

LLEWELLYN
WOODBURY, MINNESOTA

FIRST EDITION
First Printing, 2025

Book design by Samantha Peterson
Cover design by Shira Atakpu
Interior illustrations by Llewellyn Art Department

Llewellyn Publications is a registered trademark of Llewellyn Worldwide Ltd.

Library of Congress Cataloging-in-Publication Data (Pending)
ISBN: 978-0-7387-7929-4

Llewellyn Worldwide Ltd. does not participate in, endorse, or have any authority or responsibility concerning private business transactions between our
authors and the public.
   All mail addressed to the author is forwarded but the publisher cannot, unless
specifically instructed by the author, give out an address or phone number.
   Any internet references contained in this work are current at publication time,
but the publisher cannot guarantee that a specific location will continue to be
maintained. Please refer to the publisher's website for links to authors' websites
and other sources.

Llewellyn Publications
A Division of Llewellyn Worldwide Ltd.
2143 Wooddale Drive
Woodbury, MN 55125-2989
www.llewellyn.com

Printed in the United States of America

I dedicate this book to my children—Andrew, Tayllor, Jullian, and Robert—and grandchildren—Allora, Jullian, and Kisana—for whom I have worked hard to provide a new path of love and light on this journey of life.

CONTENTS

DISCLAIMER

The information provided in this trauma self-help book is for educational and informational purposes only. It is not a substitute for professional medical advice, diagnosis, or treatment. Always seek the advice of your physician or other qualified mental health provider with any questions you may have regarding a medical condition. Never disregard professional medical advice or delay in seeking it because of something you have read in this book. If you are in crisis or you think you may have a medical emergency, call your doctor or 911 immediately. The author and publisher of this book are not responsible for any specific health or mental health needs that may require medical supervision and are not liable for any damages or negative consequences from any treatment, action, application, or preparation to any person reading or following the information in this book. Common sense is strongly urged when contemplating employment of the practices and substances described in this work.

AUTHOR'S NOTE

Dear Reader,

I am glad you are here. I have been waiting a long time to share the healing power in this book with you! If, like me, you have lived with many challenges and have little to no knowledge of healing, I am here to help. If you have experienced harm in your present or past, and the lingering effects remain, you have come to the right place. I, too, was plagued by harmful experiences, ones that my mind would soon forget, but my body would continue to remember. Time and time again, my body would remind me of a past hurt—sometimes with a bruise, or even a shocking emotion. This is why I say that trauma hides; we don't always remember it, even though it lingers in the body.

Whether you are consciously aware of harmful experiences that stay with you over the years, this is the right place for healing. What this book provides for you is a way up and out of trauma responses into healing and peace. These pages lay out a strong foundation for trauma healing and living in peace. In this book, I share the exact pathway I used to identify, heal, and remove trauma responses from my life. The blueprint you'll receive is complete with real-life experiences, building blocks for growth, and healing tools.

I have shared my experiences in a step-by-step process that leads you to healing through expanding your knowledge about trauma, quick and easy activities to help move you through trauma responses, exercises that ask you to reflect, and many other tools that have yet to be compiled in one place until now. I am so grateful for my life and my healing that I wanted to share them with you. Get ready for an experience.

To get the most out of this book, I encourage you to use a journal to write in as you walk through the learnings, ponder questions, and practice the healing tools, affirmations, rituals, and activities that lie ahead. Revisit the tools in this book often, and find ways to incorporate them into your daily life. This book is a healing vehicle and you are in the driver's seat; by taking charge of your learning experience, you'll discover the greatest benefit possible.

The road ahead will challenge you; this is not a shortcut to healing. As you read and work your way through the practices and reflections, allow both space and grace for yourself. It's okay if this work takes time; set a loving pace and don't rush the process.

But be courageous, forge ahead, and know this: you are moving toward an awakening. You are not alone. I will be with you on these pages as I share my experiences, trauma coaching stories, and roads to healing. To connect with me further, visit the resource and connection page found on my website at lisaycollins .com. Reading this book is a loving act that will open your body, mind, and spirit. I wrote this book in love for all the souls carrying experiences they would like to walk away from, just as I learned to do. Take my hand as I guide you through a transformative experience to live in peace, joy, and light.

Much love,

Lisa

FOREWORD
BY CYNDI DALE

CYNDI DALE IS THE AUTHOR OF NEARLY FORTY BOOKS
ABOUT ENERGY HEALING, INCLUDING *ENERGY HEAL-
ING FOR TRAUMA, STRESS & CHRONIC ILLNESS*

Kintsugi is the Japanese art of putting broken pottery pieces back together with gold. This four-hundred-year-old technique embraces scars, which become part of the unique design. No longer marks of ugliness, these shattered shards transform into facets of beauty. From the imperfect emerges a new perfection.

The same promise of metamorphosis interweaves through Dr. Lisa Collins's brilliant book, *The Truth About Trauma*, in relation to trauma recovery. My summary of her premise is this:

You can be broken and still break free.

In other words…

You can be made whole, no matter how splintered you are.

If you have picked up this book, it's because you have experienced trauma, an injury that has caused disfigurement to your body, mind, or soul. Most likely, you've survived multiple traumas and are still reeling from them. Explains Dr. Lisa, traumatic events are those that leave adverse reactions. They are life altering. They cause anguish. And they are beyond grueling to address.

Now, I'm going to mix metaphors. Bear with me, and it will all make sense.

One of the reasons it is so difficult to recover from trauma is that when we're trying to heal, the original ordeal often spins into others. Trauma is like an intelligent and shape-shifting beast, a multiheaded hydra.

The hydra was a legendary Greek water snake with nine heads. It could not be destroyed because one of the heads was immortal. Cut a head off, and another would grow in its place. You know what that is like. Heck, I know what that is like. To heal from an alcoholic family system, I stopped drinking and doubled up on caffeine, cigarettes, and sugar instead, which I have long healed from. To boost the low self-esteem resulting from an angry mom, I entered unhealthy relationships. No matter what the core wounds in your life are, they often spur others.

In Greek mythology, Hercules ended the monster once and for all. He outsmarted it. After lobbing off a head, he cauterized the wound. Voila. He then continued his hero's journey, bettering himself to aid others.

Dr. Lisa's work can help you finish the lingering monsters of trauma. What then? You get to fill in the scars with gold glitter.

As she explains, there are lots of events that lead to trauma, the lingering impact of hardships. These include physical, emotional, mental, verbal, cultural, racial, gender-based, and spiritual hardships. As an energy healer, I know there are subtle energy causes of trauma, and Dr. Lisa speaks to these too. These maladies are subtle or psychic in nature. Their imprints are harsh and harder to address because they appear invisible to others.

Starting with science, Dr. Lisa explains why the long-term results of trauma linger so long. It is not your fault. The body really does keep the score, as contemporary researchers suggest. Yet, being *wronged* does not mean something is *wrong with you*. The great news is that Dr. Lisa has outlined the keys that can help you rewrite your story.

This is no small thing. According to the World Health Organization (WHO), about 70 percent of all people globally will experience at least one traumatic event in their lifetime.[1] At best, that figure is incomplete. Though it reveals that you are in good company, statistics aren't very useful when you're trying to rid yourself of trauma's hydra heads, including addictions, insomnia, cycles of pain and panic, low self-esteem, negative self-talk, and so much more.

Dr. Lisa's protocol is clean and straightforward in that it involves three foundational levels of healing. In short, these are carrying out bodily care, changing destructive mind patterns, and applying beneficial healing tools. The latter medicine kit is chock-full, and the processes work. Meditation, breathing, energy healing, nature, music. Who knew that recovery could be so enjoyable?

You'll need to be diligent, but your self-devotion will evolve into self-love. You must give the process time, but you'll learn you are worth it. Throughout, you will be attended by the sage master and mystic that is Dr. Lisa.

---

1. World Health Organization, "Post-Traumatic Stress Disorder," May 27, 2024, https://www.who.int/news-room/fact-sheets/detail/post-traumatic -stress-disorder#:~:text=Around%2070%25%20of%20people%20globally,in %20their%20lives%20(2).

I can't say enough about how much I respect her at every level. Her personhood embodies integrity. Her professionalism is world renowned. She has summarized the wisdom of transformation, and it all lies within this book.

And now, it is time to become the masterpiece—and legend—you really are.

INTRODUCTION

The Truth About Trauma is a guide to healing. This book demystifies trauma through three practical learning levels that reveal how to identify traumatic experiences in our bodies and minds to heal. The truth is our body holds trauma. Once we acknowledge this, we can uncover the related belief systems that keep the energy of trauma trapped in our body and keep us stuck in the feelings and thoughts of trauma responses. Uncovering and shifting our belief systems allows us to create new paths to break free from trauma and live in peace.

You'll learn how to transform harmful energy into positive energy as you walk through three levels of healing:

- Level 1: Body Sensations
- Level 2: Mind Patterns
- Level 3: Reflective Tools, Positive Reconnection with Body, Mind, and Spirit

My journey to learning about trauma began with looking for ways to live a more resilient lifestyle. I found myself feeling disconnected from people I loved, having mood swings, and being quickly and overly irritated by many daily incidents. For years, I had thought this was simply my personality type; things bothered me. Somewhere along the way, I stumbled onto the fact that I could not control or explain my irritations, and, sometimes, I could not shake them off.

I found that science was unequivocal on how the body and brain worked to protect the body. Learning about the body and its responses assisted me in paying attention to physical responses connected to traumatic experiences that continued to live in my body. My first step in learning about trauma was to realize how strong reactions in the body could be rooted in past negative experiences, which we'll cover in Level 1: Body Sensations.

Something else I noticed is how I continually brought more and more activities into my life. I could not settle myself down to enjoy life without doing more. I was in constant motion, which meant my thinking was in constant motion too. I needed to be settled or calmed down. In this state, I had difficulty answering how I felt about things. My self-talk was negative. I would think negatively about my actions and body or, in general, criticize myself. It was the examination of my negative thoughts that assisted me in replacing them with positive ones. This is the process that I'll walk you through in Level 2. The reflection of conscious and subconscious thoughts is the foundation of our work in Level 2.

I found that noticing what was happening in my body and reflecting on conscious and subconscious thoughts provided more comfort to my life. Suddenly, I did not feel plagued by the same feelings and ideas from previous traumatic experiences. In

Level 3, I continued to maintain growth by acknowledging and reflecting regularly, increasing the quality of my life, and having a positive outlook. These regular action steps helped me reconnect with my body, mind, and spiritual well-being. The maintenance steps you'll experience in Level 3 are designed to support your reconnection with body, mind, and spirit.

The Truth About Trauma will teach you about what trauma is and why we must pay attention to its responses. Trauma is a physical response to a threat; these responses live within our nervous system. The body remembers these frightening experiences and records them to keep us safe. These experiences are threads in the fabric of our beings. When we look at ourselves as if we were a handcrafted piece of cloth, we see the beautiful soul we are; yet when something pulls a thread, we can respond out of sorts. Looking closely at this response is where we'll find the code to unlock the experiences holding us back.

The Truth About Trauma provides a learning, discovery, and reflection system. The three levels of education provide a guidepost for interrupting traumatic responses and replacing them with positive energy.

Overall, this book will provide hope for healing trauma. Once trauma is understood and recognized, one can heal. When trauma energy is healed, positive vital energy can flow into the mind, body, and spirit of those seeking more peace and rejuvenation from past harms and experiences.

This three-level approach to trauma healing is grounded in my profound experiences of seeking to understand and heal from past traumas, which for me include physical and sexual abuse, addiction, and depression. As a result, I have sought inner peace by restoring my body, mind, and spirit. The approach outlined in the book, while grounded in my journey, has led to transformative experiences for others I have supported as an educator, life coach, and trauma healing practitioner. Healing has expanded my life tenfold; dreams continue to come true. I believe that healing my trauma made room for magical opportunities in my life. I can see the opportunities because I have cleared my life to receive them.

Trauma is always talked about but rarely explained in a way that one can understand and move toward healing. My work in trauma healing for organizations and individuals has been transformative for me as a professional and for many others I've had the privilege to support on this journey. I first encountered trauma healing work as an educational director when I attended a workshop in Lancaster, Pennsylvania, Amish country. The training was at a satellite campus of the Eastern Mennonite University, and little did I know that the Mennonites had a long history of bringing care to those who suffered. In hindsight, what brought me to the training is mystical because that training has changed my life and continues to uplift the lives of many others.

I was interested in the training because it was about trauma and resilience. Hardly ever will you hear about resilience, but trauma is blaring in the airways. My interest as an education director in a school district was to learn how to support educators in increasing resilience for themselves, their students, and the students' families. I signed up for the training, was accepted, and traveled to learn more.

As an educational leader, I was familiar with sitting in training to learn about all kinds of subjects; therefore, I prepared myself for long days of somewhat boring content. The first day literally took my breath away. I found myself in a room full of strangers. Each person worked in a helping profession in a different part of the world. The group included a pastor and his wife from the Midwest who were missionaries in a Haitian village. Another man came from Switzerland, and he was an ambulance driver who had originally lived in Africa. He fled from his African home because of all the violence he witnessed. Also present was a nurse who had worked in war-torn African countries, trying to save lives. She had been escorted by the military out of those countries for her safety. One African man was a peacebuilder during war and unrest. He had witnessed whole families being executed and buried in his country. He was there to learn more about processing trauma and peacebuilding.

Hearing the stories of the people in attendance took my breath away. The stories they shared as they introduced themselves were happening worldwide. As they spoke, I looked past the news stories and media posts into the events and experiences themselves. Trauma was not only real on a global level but also on a personal level for each person in attendance. Seeing this, my original intention of picking up a few tips about trauma and how to teach resilience in my school district faded away. I was no longer simply attending a training on trauma. Suddenly, I was experiencing a change in my own life as I learned what trauma was and what it was not. The instructor told us that trauma occurred in the body, and one of the first signs is a reduction of breath. When threatened, she said that our breathing becomes shallow. I did not believe it at first, but as I listened to the stories, I noticed I was hardly taking in oxygen. She said that trauma happens in the body and that the body responds to protect itself through flight, fight, or freeze, and I had just learned that firsthand by experiencing the sensations myself. I discovered a lot about myself on that first day of training; specifically, I learned that sensations I had not paid attention to or had ignored were trauma responses. The facilitator was right.

As the training progressed, I learned more information about trauma and how, why, and when it occurred. The most important thing I learned was how to interrupt it. Although I did not attend the training to reflect on what may be unhealed in my life, what happened is that I discovered I was living with unhealed trauma, and there was a path toward healing.

Upon this discovery, I became a sponge; I listened, took notes, and learned all I could. The aspiration from learning about trauma was to be free from it and the energy of it in my life, both consciously and unconsciously. The realization for me was that I was a survivor of many harms as a child, and in turn, I developed survival skills that did not center myself, my needs, wants, or desires. I was missing a piece of my puzzle to living a happy, peaceful life. My body, mind, and spirit were not peaceful. A constant hum of stress coursed through my body like a revving engine. Inside my body, I responded to life; my stomach would get tight, I would hold my breath, and I would instantly be angry at someone for causing an obstacle. Without introspection, I could not clearly see how to solve my issues.

A huge turning point for me was a doctor's visit when I was directed to take time off from work. The doctor was earnest. I was in physical trouble, and I did not recognize it. I needed healing. How I held stress in my body, mind, and spirit was how I lived. I did not have to live that way, and neither do you.

Self-reflection of body, mind, and spirit helped me reclaim freedom. I discovered knowledge about myself, and more importantly, I learned a way to view trauma responses in my body, allowing me to create a roadmap on how to release the past to find peace within.

Throughout the years following that first training program, I learned much about the truth about trauma and the tools to heal body, mind, and spirit. My journey has taken me to unexpected heights; I had no idea I was creating a roadmap. I now know the combination of tools I used for my own healing can be used as a healing roadmap for anyone.

My healing began with changing the responses in my body by reflecting on how and where a feeling originated. Over time, I began to feel, love, and care for myself. The effort has been more than worth it.

This book is a testament to my journey. I share the steps I traveled to connect with my body, remove all negative ideas, and release new energy into my body, mind, and spirit.

At its core, this book shares scientific information about trauma and how it affects our bodies. However, it will take you far beyond obtaining knowledge; it will teach, guide, and help you move beyond the emotional imprisonment of past trauma. It will guide you through the process of breaking free from trauma and restoring positive energy to your life. Using my life as a map and example, you will see what I did to help myself as you reflect and take similar actions.

How I entered the healing space is mystical, but what happened to my life from the healing I have experienced is miraculous! As each opportunity for healing came into my life, I said yes to it. I was ready, and although I did not believe in some things that came my way, I tried them, and I encourage you to do the same. I am so glad I did. I live a free life today and did not know

I needed it. With the knowledge of trauma awareness in my life, I believe I heightened my desire for the universe to heal me.

I really thought I knew myself, but the shocking thing is I did not. The more I found out that my experiences, positive and negative, influenced how I showed up in the world, the more I wanted to interrupt the things that did not serve me. As I healed, more opportunities for healing came my way. On my journey, I was introduced to many healing methods and modalities, along with the vastness of spirituality. More and more, my life expanded into my authentic self and the joy life offers.

Most of us have lived a life of ups and downs, but with healing and uncovering the truth about trauma, you can live in freedom and happiness, even joy and bliss, and do not have to be defined by the winds of your past.

How the Book Is Structured

This book is designed to walk you through the healing levels sequentially. By reading the chapters in order, you will connect to the material from the beginning to the end. Each chapter is the foundation for the next chapter. As you journey through the book, you will encounter prompts, reflections, and self-care tools that are designed to provide support for your learning and exploration. The healing tools throughout the book are accompanied by real-life stories to illustrate how to use them. This book is reflective and encourages journaling throughout its pages. Pick out your favorite kind of journal for the road ahead. To assist you in continuing your healing long after you finish reading the book, an index of all the self-care tools is located in the Wellness Tool Kit at the back of the book.

I am excited for the road ahead! Here's where this journey will lead you.

To start, chapter 1 will describe trauma definitions and provide information and examples of various trauma experiences. This vital information is foundational for discussions in chapters to come. It is an essential grounding of knowledge about trauma. It will be critical in assisting you in understanding situations and incidents in your life.

Chapter 2 will deepen the discussion from chapter 1 by providing specific guidance on how to identify and heal trauma in your body. This chapter, along with all the following chapters, will also provide self-care tools, resources, and exercises to get you started on building your Wellness Tool Kit.

Chapter 3 will start with a study on how the body responds to traumatic experiences. We'll then look at how the nervous system protects the body from harmful situations. This chapter adroitly highlights those subtle forms of trauma and how the cycles of trauma responses can look and feel in one's life to help you start identifying where trauma may be hidden in your life.

Chapter 4 will include an overview of the three levels of learning about trauma experiences: body sensations, mind patterns, and reconnection tools for positive reconnection to body, mind, and spirit. This chapter will also focus on understanding connections to body sensations through the utilization of additional reflection prompts and self-care tools.

Chapter 5 builds upon the previous chapter's learning about body sensations and the relationship between mind patterns, including thoughts and belief systems. Various reflective tools will assist in exploring conscious and subconscious thoughts to discover and interrupt negative thinking.

Chapter 6 will include information about how to integrate your new learning about trauma in the body and mind into regular self-care. This chapter provides a healing roadmap and additional self-reflection and care tools to continue paving new roads of healing, strengthening, and breaking free from past trauma to continue new avenues of wellness.

Lastly, chapter 7 rounds out the discussion with a guided tour of my healing journey in several areas. Specifically, I'll show you how I used the tools and reflective exercises within the three levels of healing to share about how I healed trauma in my family system, as well as the areas of abuse, addiction, race and gender discrimination, and sexual identity trauma.

CHAPTER ONE
WHAT IS TRAUMA?

To heal from trauma, we must start in the body. Specifically, this chapter is focused on helping you understand how the body and trauma are interconnected, through sharing both lived experiences and some relevant science. The body is the place that responds to traumatic experiences. Trauma is fluid. It ebbs and flows. And everyone reacts to it differently. Once you become in touch with your body, you'll be able to recognize the energy centers where trauma might be lodged and bring that trauma to healing. The work of recognizing and removing trauma can be a challenge because it requires reliving the past harms. You may not want to believe or address a hurtful time in your life, but it is necessary for healing. Challenge yourself, pull back the covers, and examine the truth. Though painful, the process is essential for deep healing.

The body does not lie; it's the roadmap to healing. For instance, if you find tight muscles in the back and shoulders and butterflies in the stomach pretty consistently, these could be signs of past distress. Although there are many ways to deal with stress, the stress discussed here is when a harmful event happens, and the memory never leaves your body. Hints that an event has not left your body can be feeling the event as if it is occurring again, such as intense anger, sadness, shutting down, or disassociation.

What is essential to understand is that your body has been through experiences in your life, and it's your body's job to protect you from anything perceived as harmful. Discovering these buried experiences can be challenging, as they are sometimes stored deep within for many years. By examination of early childhood, school, and adulthood, you can respond to life and process unhealed emotions. This examination does not have to be a deep, therapeutic dive; it's sufficient to even simply acknowledge what has happened and what may be healthy or unhealthy experiences in your life. Ultimately, you want to heal these energies, but first, you must admit they exist. Reconciling this truth is where the rubber meets the road; we must first admit that harm occurred and possibly was caused by people you love. It is a challenge subconsciously, and it is important to face it and not pull the blinds down in denial. The idea that caretakers may have been the ones to hurt you can be difficult to accept. When you begin to examine your experiences, you might find this to feel nearly impossible. When I first started looking into my harmful experiences, I wanted to paint a picture of my parents and other caretakers doing a great job raising me. It was difficult to move into healing by acknowledgment of harm in family systems.

Many people experience harmful situations in their upbringing and life, which then become lodged in their energy centers or chakras. These experiences color how you view, process, and respond to everyday situations. I would not have believed this had I not discovered it in the work that will be outlined in this book. Everything I learned will be shared in ways you can digest, from the resistance of change to the joy of peace. It is all part of the process. If it were easy to unearth these experiences, everyone would jump on the bandwagon—no one would have any unhealed trauma! The most challenging part of change is realizing that a problem exists. When trauma is exposed, it is the beginning of healing. Many tools brought healing to my life. In these pages, you will learn about trauma and, most importantly, how to heal. My healing journey allowed me to experience tools that span from life coaching tools, energy medicine, belief work, interpersonal neurobiology, and more to help me understand and deepen my healing.

Because there is a mountain of information and supportive modalities, knowing where to start can feel overwhelming. Here, as our first step is to bring awareness to potentially harmful events and learn more about how trauma is stored in the body, we'll begin by looking at adverse childhood experiences (ACES). ACES involve life-changing challenges like violence, abuse, or neglect that occur in childhood. This category of experiences also includes when a child is exposed to a family member dying, struggling with mental illness or addiction, or spending time in jail or prison. ACES originates from a research study by medical doctors at Kaiser Permanente from 1995 to 1997 where adults taking an annual physical exam were asked questions about their childhood. Seventeen thousand people completed the questions on childhood experiences, and researchers found that adults who experienced ACES indicated adult health issues. Of the participants in the survey, one ACE was reported by two-thirds of the participants, and more than three ACES were reported by one in five participants.[1] This research study showed that experiencing ACES correlates to health problems. Any ACE increases the likelihood of health problems like injury (traumatic brain injury, fractures, or burns), mental health (depression, anxiety, or suicide), maternal health (unintended pregnancy, pregnancy complications, or fetal death), infectious disease (HIV or STDs), chronic disease (cancer or diabetes), risky behavior (alcohol and drug abuse, unsafe sex, or opioid misuse), and missed opportunities (related to education, occupation, or income).

As you're starting to see, ACES affect many of life's building blocks. Let's start by personally examining the ACES test questions. Answer yes or no to the following statements about your childhood. A simple yes or no answers the question, and then the total number of yeses is counted, which is your score. According to the research, the larger the score, the more risk of sickness and emotional problems one may experience in adulthood. The score measures the stress you grew up with as a child.

If you are not ready to take the test, do not force yourself to do so. Take it when you feel prepared. It is okay to skip the test and come back to it. The important part of this activity is to reflect on your early life. If you can already think of something that feels like a jagged edge for you, get out your journal and make a note. Then return to this section to answer the questions when you feel ready.

Awareness of Trauma: ACES Questions

Review the following list of experiences and make a note of any you had before eighteen years old.

---

1. Felitti, *Relationship of Childhood Abuse and Household Dysfunction*.

- Parents or caregivers swore at me.
- Parents or caregivers pushed, grabbed, or threw things at me.
- I experienced sexual abuse by someone five or more years older than me.
- I was hungry.
- My parents divorced.
- I witnessed my parent, stepparent, or caretaker being pushed or hit by another adult.
- There were problems with drinking or street drugs.
- There were problems in my household of depression, mental illness, or suicide attempts.
- Someone in my home went to jail or prison.

This test was one of my first indicators that my childhood was not the fairy tale I had painted it to be. Reflect on your answers to these questions and how many you answered yes to. It is okay to be sad about the results. What we don't want to do is ignore it. Ignoring and moving on means the trauma and stress will continue to live in your body. Admitting the truth of situations in the ACES test can be challenging.

The ACES exposure gave me the courage to look deeper into past childhood experiences. Examination of ACES propelled the steps needed for healing. Through this one exercise, you can start the process necessary to heal, forgive, and move on with your life. Past experiences can color your personality and how you show up in the world. The energy from your childhood treatment does not need to follow you around the rest of your life and inform you how to treat, respond, and engage with other people. You can begin the healing process once you begin working on childhood and adulthood traumatic experiences.

The same idea of recognizing, healing, and moving forward goes for adulthood experiences. Like childhood events, adulthood experiences can leave the residue of trauma and trap negative energy in your body. Suppose you have experienced abuse in a relationship with a coworker, supervisor, friend, romantic partner, or family member. That event may still be with you. If you have survived or witnessed a traumatic accident, the event may still be with you. Any experience in which your body has felt danger holds the potential to internalize the negative energy that fuels a trauma response.

Addiction and Other Harmful Challenges

In addition to life experiences, another indication of harm being stored in your body is addiction. If you have suffered any form of addiction, obsessive behavior, or lack of caring for yourself, it is an area that requires attention.

In my early adulthood, I fell into addiction and an unhealthy marriage. The choices I made in these early years of my life were unhealthy, accompanied by an array of up-and-down emotions and feelings. I did not have the awareness to acknowledge or process how I felt during these years. Harm from these times needed to be examined and healed.

For this next exercise, think back to your early teenage years, as these years tend to be challenging for nearly everyone. What you are looking for here are the events that, when you think about them, bring about feelings from that time.

Use the list below to assist you in thinking about times in your life. Feel free to make notes in your journal as you go down the list.

- Relationship
- Workaholism
- Abuse
- Addiction
- Children planned or unplanned
- Homelessness
- Military participation
- Victim of violence: mental, physical, or emotional
- Bullying
- Domestic violence
- Silenced emotions
- Intergenerational trauma
- Addictions
- Self-abuse
- Physical ailments
- Repetitive conflicts
- Accidents
- Fires
- Car accidents
- Threatening behavior by you
- Rage/anger
- Extreme sadness

- Depression
- PTSD

Review areas of your life and reflect on times when there were both challenges and joys. Joyful moments are essential to capture during this process as well. Our lives have challenges and joys; seeing where life is joyful is important. Using your journal, jot down some thoughts that appear from the writing prompts below:

- Think of memories in your life where you experienced joy.
- Describe memories in your life where you experienced challenges.

It is vital to see your threads of experience. These threads come together for your healing journey. Examining the issues that have been put away for safekeeping is part of the process. A characteristic of trauma is that it is hidden until something comes near to activate it. You may not realize it's there, but when activated, you may notice changes in mood, sudden unexplained feelings, extreme feelings, or a lack of control. Each person responds differently; it is important to note all your experiences on this journey.

Are you in relationships that are not healthy and continue to cause ongoing conflict? Those relationships can be in your family system, work environment, or neighborhood. If you have felt trapped in circumstances, it is something to examine. Whether you processed, shared, or discussed these feelings previously does not matter. If there is a part of your life where a lack of self-love or self-care has shown up as deep-rooted neglect, this is an area to examine. It does not matter how minor the issue may be; it is essential to note it. Part of your consciousness will want to dismiss everything and say it was not that bad. The truth about trauma is it hides to protect you. It will take courage to examine the joy and the sorrow of your experiences.

Journal Reflection: Your Experiences

You learned more about your experiences in this section. In your journal, in addition to your challenges and joyful moments, write about your reflections and wonderings from this section.

Real-Life Experiences Shared

As a Conscious Freedom Life Coach, trauma practitioner, and organizational consultant, I am trained to examine the shadow or root causes of life challenges to help heal them. I look for signs of trauma responses to support others in breaking free from the responses and healing the harm that caused the response. My work in organizations is grounded in the examinations of harmful practices and supporting individuals and systems toward healthy change.

Throughout the book, I will share examples of real-life experiences to help ground the work we're doing in everyday reality, which will assist you with relating to the processes of using the level system for healing.

Note that, within the real-life examples I share, the names and identities of the individuals who sought my professional guidance have been changed for the purpose of this book.

> *Sue worked in a law office. She worked very hard to acquire her job and education. Sue's colleague and peer commented that another coworker was inadequate for the job. Sue went into a rage and verbally abused the coworker. Sue was put on leave from work, and her job*

was in jeopardy. In a session to discuss the incident, Sue admitted that she had acted inappropriately. During the discussion, Sue became rude, avoided questions, and spoke sharply. After the sudden change in mood, I asked to speak to adult Sue. This question paused Sue, and she slowly began to be herself. After a discussion, Sue shared that she'd had a difficult time around sixteen years old. Sue lived in an alcohol-addictive home and lost her mother to suicide. The coworker's words reminded Sue of the social worker who came to take her to foster care. The coworker's phrasing, attitude, and tone rhythm returned Sue to that age. Adult Sue's body responded to her coworker as a sixteen-year-old in grief and pain.

The trauma lodged in Sue's body was not removed; it was awakened by memories of the incident in her workplace. Sue could go back and start healing her sixteen-year-old self, but she was unaware the healing needed to happen until her work incident. It was a gigantic step toward a better life.

If you are facing major challenges, you need to address them head-on. You may require additional support from other practitioners or professionals. This book can act as an excellent guide to support you wherever you are in your self-love journey. Remember, what's most important is that major challenges are addressed. In my life, that is when the road toward freedom and away from trauma began to open.

Trauma from Childhood Conditioning

The first step to getting in touch with yourself is knowing your body. The following tools, like the ACES test, will assist you in your exploration. The first tool to help you self-explore is the work of Cheri Huber—a Zen student, teacher, and writer—from her book *There Is Nothing Wrong with You: Going Beyond Self-Hate*. The title alone says it all! In the book, Huber discusses how the conditioning that occurs in childhood can project that something is wrong with you. Huber states, "You have been taught that there is something wrong with you and that you are imperfect, but there isn't and you're not."[2] She illustrates that many adults have lived through a childhood that becomes the foundation of self-hatred. The author begins the book with a litany of phrases said to children. Alone, only one or two of the phrases she lists will not raise an eyebrow, but the list in its entirety will take your breath away. At least that is what happened when I read them. Here's a sample:

> *Don't do that…stop that…put that down…I told you not to do that…why don't you ever listen…wipe that look off your face…I'll give you something to cry about…*

If you can imagine hearing these kinds of phrases over and over again, then you can see how it would easily take a toll on the mind, body, and spirit. These phrases are just a few from a long list of things said to children in frustration. Children are young souls who are vulnerable and innocent. As children, each of us formulates a way to see the world. A hard snarl of "that serves you right" is packed with harmful implications for a youngster. Huber states many people, upon hearing these phrases, believe that something has to be wrong with them, or why else would people treat them that way.

---

2. Huber, *There Is Nothing Wrong with You.*

Now, not everyone grew up with challenging childhoods or in an environment where they heard a long list of hurtful phrases, but at some point in your journey, at least one adult probably said something that hurt. The hurt that does not go away is trauma. Any action in language, gesture, or physical treatment that is harmful can be lodged in the memory and body.

Huber, a Zen Buddhist monk, found that in her practice of working with people, she needed to help them find themselves by undoing the conditioning of their childhood. Huber states that spiritual practice is necessary to go beyond self-hatred. In this book, the practice involves getting in touch with your body first and then your mind to connect to the spirit clearly. The flow of the body, mind, and spirit connection is necessary to remove the harm or trauma that lingers within. Huber's book is an excellent on-ramp for connecting with body and mind.

As you reflect on the foundation of your life and beyond, you will discover areas of resilience and areas where healing can take place. You may notice things you have not noticed before. We're not trying to put a microscope on parenting, but rather, our intent is to focus on self-healing from actions, statements, and general ways of being that did not serve you as a human being and continue to cause issues in your life consciously and subconsciously. We have all heard the statement that our parents or caretakers did the best they could at the time. What we do not hear much about is the thoughts, words, and actions of generational trauma passed from generation to generation. Evidence of past generational harm coming into the present can be seen in how children are treated. How children are spoken to directly impacts the growth of self-esteem and self-worth. Young souls' psychological and emotional wellness begins with loving and sometimes unloving interactions. This will not be the case for all, but what is a universal experience for those with trauma lodged in their body is an experience or experiences that did not sit well, which left a negative residue in their system.

Making Room for Feelings: Pete's Experience

Trauma responses can come from smells, touches, sounds, perceptions, or sudden memories that seem like threats or reactions from past experiences. It is hard to believe that the body responding to threats is a manifestation of trauma. Often, you may think you are overreacting; there is always a reason for what is happening. Day-to-day living can include responses to past traumas lingering in the body. These reactions are so subtle that you may believe it's your personality. It can be shocking to find out that many attributes are coping strategies from past experiences. Here's an example showing Pete's experience with managing feelings.

Pete grew up in a home where discussing feelings was frowned upon and discouraged. At a young age, he was told, "I don't care about your feelings." Pete always remembered that statement. His family would tease him if he said how he felt. His ability to process his feelings and share were limited. As a result, Pete could not process his feelings and those of others. He was unaware that he had a block around acknowledging how he felt or how others felt. Pete would ignore how others felt and was unable to accept, show empathy, or be supportive of the feelings of others. When a friend or close relationship would share their feelings, Pete would listen, but he could not validate their feelings, comfort them, or celebrate them. Pete was emotionally flat in his expressions of how he dealt with emotions, which led to challenging relationships in and outside work.

Challenges in work-related and romantic relationships motivated Pete to seek help. He was searching for a solution. In the coaching sessions, Pete remembered how his family made fun of him for having feelings by using the Thinking Map (a tool we'll cover later in this book). Using the tool, he recognized that his actions were grounded in what he had learned growing up: there is no room for feelings. While using this reflective tool, Pete examined a situation at work. The energy of his early childhood experience affected all his romantic and otherwise relationships. Looking more closely at this early incident, Pete could return to reconcile his feelings. Pete used the tool to remove shame; he also used the forgiveness tool (covered later in this book). Pete returned to this memory and healed it so he would not be plagued by not processing his feelings and emotionally acting differently for himself and others.

The catalyst for Pete discovering this information about himself was his feelings of discomfort in relationships and issues at work. He was an attentive and supportive person, yet when asked how he felt, he was stuck. He was like a brick wall when it came to discussing how he felt. This stiffness and detachedness from his feelings did not feel right to him. His body would tense when others spoke of emotions or shared intense feelings. Instead of blaming them for being over the top, Pete began to look for a root cause. Through journaling and meditation, he found the one harmful statement: *I don't care about your feelings.* As an adult, Pete chose not to continue to relive this harm. Just as Pete learned, identification of trauma will require being in touch with your body and mind.

The Science of Trauma

Science has substantiated that trauma lives in the body. Trauma is a physical response to something that seems like a threat. It is not an emotional response, nor can it be controlled by only thinking differently. The event will linger and hide in the body like a bruise if it is strong enough. When a threat occurs, the rational part of your brain takes a seat, and the emotional part of your brain takes charge. Imagine for a minute that the emotional part of your brain is running the show. That sounds like a messy situation, right? When the threat seemingly has passed, the rational brain comes back online and takes over. Use this lens when you see a person struggling in anger or tears—what part of the brain is in charge?

In addition to the rational brain taking a break, our breathing becomes shallow, which means less oxygen is getting to the brain, further constricting our capacity to adapt to the situation. All of this happens in a short time. So short of a time, in fact, that we do not notice and continue as if nothing has occurred.

If strong enough, the event will linger and hide in the body like a sore. This sore becomes part of your implicit and explicit memories; it becomes part of you. In doing so, part of your body wants to protect you from further harm, so the event's soreness or memory is isolated from other experiences unless something comes too close. Your instincts work to protect you by providing a subconscious reaction to anything that the body perceives as a threat. You may find yourself seemingly overreacting or experiencing other responses (flight, fight, fawn, or flock) without much understanding why.

For example, I reacted very strongly during an experience when I was touched on the upper bicep on a date.

"Do not put your hands on me!" I snapped.

My reaction was extreme, and I had no idea why I acted that way. My date assured me no harm was intended. I was unaware that my reaction was a response to trauma. I did not recall being grabbed as a child, but my body did.

When the body responds to an experience that triggers our trauma, stress hormones flood our system to help us fight off the danger. Can you imagine, time after time, continued stress hormones flooding your body without any release? The overproduction of stress hormones in our bodies produces a reverse effect of efficiency. Instead of responding like it should when you're in danger, your body overreacts at the slightest concern and has difficulty getting back to calm. This response and calming cycle depletes the body, mind, and spirit.

Many authors have written about this response. In this book, you will see the alignment of these writings to explore healing that will bring the most benefit to your health. *Energy Healing for Stress and Chronic Illness* by internationally renowned author, speaker, healer, and business consultant Cyndi Dale extensively describes how traumatic experiences affect the body's energetic health. Dale states that trauma produces chronic problems and experiences, which can lead to physical responses. Dale continues to connect the relationship between subtle anatomy, such as organs, channels, and energy fields, and physical trauma responses. Harmful experiences relate to every part of our being.

In *Trauma Stewardship*, Laura van Dernoot Lipsky, founder and director of the Trauma Stewardship Institute and author of *Trauma Stewardship: An Everyday Guide to Caring for Self While Caring for Others* and *The Age of Overwhelm*, shares sixteen warning signs of exposure to trauma. Lipsky shares these warning signs because the connection to the realization of trauma in our body is hard to acknowledge. The very nature of trauma is that it becomes part of our body system to protect us.

Peter Levine is the author of several bestselling books on trauma. In *An Unspoken Voice: How the Body Releases Trauma and Restores Goodness,* Levine states that the body responds to trauma with resilience. Levine says resolved trauma occurs when fear can be separated from feeling stuck.

Carolyn Yoder, an international trauma and resilience trainer and a Licensed Professional Counselor (LPC) specializing in finding ways to move toward healing and peace, is the author of *Strategies for Trauma Awareness and Resilience* (STAR). Yoder states that unhealed trauma creates a cycle of responses in the body and actions toward others or internally toward oneself. Yoder named this response to trauma the "cycles of violence."[3] Yoder describes various actions and reactions to trauma that can continue, an ongoing, never-ending response from one response to another. The trauma responses can range from depression to continued conflicts with others.

Knowledge about trauma is only the first step in this recovery process. Each of these authors is correct; trauma appears in our bodies, systems, and energies. However, the body's natural response to a traumatic experience is to find safety. Finding safety can look like getting away from a situation that is uncomfortable (flight). Another example of safety is digging your heels in to push back in a situation (fight). If a situation is uncomfortable, you may find yourself wanting to be in the company of a group (flock) to feel better. In some situations, you may find yourself

---

3. Yoder, *The Little Book of Trauma Healing.*

looking for favor or closeness with the person who is the cause of the harm (fawn) to protect yourself. However you take action to be comfortable in day-to-day life, you may not realize that this response is from trauma. The journey toward healing is recognizing an event that may still be lingering in our systems and using the tools outlined to heal the memory through the body, mind, and spirit connection.

Expanding Understanding through Interpersonal Neurobiology

Interpersonal neurobiology (IPNB) embraces all branches of science to expand understanding of the mind, body, and brain in connection with relationships. According to Dan Siegel, a clinical psychiatry professor at UCLA School of Medicine and the director of the Mindsight Institute, the working knowledge of IPNB "explores how relationships and the brain interact to shape our mental lives."[4] IPNB states that the mind, relationships, and the brain create one system. The key to IPNB is relationships. Relationships mold how we process, understand, and react to life. Through a year-long study of IPNB, I learned how to relate to others based on my interactions. This point is so important: I believed there was something universally wrong with me, and there was nothing wrong with me. I am the result of the meaningful relationships in my life. This means that without knowing it, you can adopt actions, thoughts, and ways that are not necessarily how you want to behave but have been programmed to. I understood this best when I learned how my nervous system learned to process life. In IPNB, this is discussed in the form of attachments.

---

4. Siegel, *Pocket Guide to Interpersonal Neurobiology*.

The Four Attachment Styles

I learned about four attachment styles: secure, ambivalent, avoidant, and disorganized. This learning had a mighty influence on me. Much like the other learning and healing I have done, this layer of learning assisted me in understanding my foundations.

Attachments refer to your first relationships with your caregivers as a child. These connections can predict adult connections and relationships.

Secure attachment represents a parent or caregiver the child sees as protection, a comforter, and a steadfast provider. Dan Siegel says the child views them as seen, soothed, and safe. Adults with secure attachment have healthier relationships; are comfortable with intimacy; have good coping and problem-solving skills; communicate effectively; are comfortable being alone and close; are trusting, empathetic, and compassionate; and can regulate emotions and feelings. Those qualities are extraordinary!

I did not start with those qualities in adulthood. I have degrees in them now and need to continue working at them. Before learning IPNB, I had not heard of attachments. Based on the former description, I did not have a secure attachment. This fact is not about blame. It is about becoming a healthier me and a healthier you. If you find challenges in the attributes of secure attachments, be curious to look deeper at healing those foundations.

Take time here to reflect on the attributes of secure attachment. Consider the attributes you have in your life; write in your journal what qualities you possess.

- Healthy relationships
- Comfortable with intimacy
- Good coping skills

- Problem-solving skills
- Communicates effectively
- Comfortable being alone
- Being close
- Trusting
- Empathetic
- Compassionate
- Regulates emotions and feelings

Describe in your journal areas you would like to shift.

Ambivalent attachment is when the caretaker is inconsistent, and the child experiences unresolved conflict from the on-again, off-again care. The child is unsure if they will be cared for or be safe. They may feel separation anxiety or emotional distress when the parent is absent. Adults who have experienced ambivalent attachment may have a fear of abandonment, be needy and clingy, have mood swings, have intense anxiety in relationships, and have difficulty with emotional and physical boundaries. If you find yourself moving between needing and loving people and not needing and loving them, this may be something to examine.

Take time here to reflect on the attributes of ambivalent attachment. In your journal, describe the qualities that feel familiar to you.

- Fear of abandonment
- Needy and clingy
- Mood swings
- Moving between loving and ignoring loved ones
- Intense anxiety in relationships

- Difficulty with emotions
- Difficulty with physical boundaries

Reflect on the areas you would like to shift.

Avoidant attachment is when the child feels uncomfortable being around the caregiver. The parent may be scary or not emotionally available, so the child does not seek closeness to the parent or caregiver yet prefers being alone. An adult who has experienced an avoidant attachment avoids connection with loved ones, is unavailable emotionally to their children, does not long for loved ones, avoids confrontation, has difficulty expressing emotions, and does not seek company.

This one took a lot of work to write about. I see some of these attributes in myself. The hardest part of this work is admitting that once that happens, the healing can start. If you identify with this attachment, you are not alone. Know that there is a way to get up and out of these feelings. The tools shared later in the book in Level 2: Mind Patterns and Level 3: Reflection Tools will assist you in making sense of attachments. Take time here to reflect on the attributes for avoidant attachment. Describe the qualities of avoidant attachment that feel familiar to you in your journal.

- Avoids connection with loved ones
- Unavailable emotionally to their children
- Does not long for loved ones
- Avoids confrontation
- Hard time expressing emotions
- Does not seek company

Describe in your journal the areas you would like to shift.

The last attachment is the *disorganized attachment*. In this attachment, the child fears being too close to the caregiver. The child does not feel safe based on their experience with physical or emotional abuse. The child may also exhibit aggression when near the parent or caregiver. The child has difficulty calming oneself, may feel confused, and may not feel connected to self or others. An adult who has experienced disorganization attachment is afraid of intimacy and vulnerability, can be rageful when confronted, lacks empathy, and suffers from a lack of personal boundaries.

I identify with this attachment as well. It is difficult to put the pieces together that disorganized attachment could drastically affect adulthood. The year-long IPBN course was taught in a caring fashion. The facilitators loved us, made us comfortable, and created a true trauma-informed environment while we learned and accepted facts about ourselves so we could go out and help others. I have not had such a warm and loving environment since.

This book aims to uncover harm and discard hurt to transform it into healing. If you identify with disorganized attachment, this could be the first step in understanding the why of your challenges. If you are not feeling well, maybe sick to your stomach, or feeling like you need a nap after reading this, your body is communicating with you. That happened to me in this work. Take a break and soothe yourself. Get a glass of tea, find a comfortable place to rest, and call a friend to talk to. The way this information hit my body was hard because there was truth there. I had to breathe deeply and let myself grieve for the child who had suffered. I could not live there, but I had to do it, and I did not do it alone. If this hits you hard, contact your support team to be with you. All this work requires support; take time to use your resources.

When you are ready, take time to reflect on the attributes for disorganized attachment. Describe the qualities that feel familiar to you in your journal.

- Afraid of intimacy
- Lacks vulnerability
- Rageful when confronted
- Lacks empathy
- Suffers from lack of personal boundaries

Reflect on the areas you would like to shift. What support system do you have in place in your life?

Implicit and Explicit Memories

Trauma lives in our bodies through implicit and explicit memories. The saying that the body keeps the score means that the body remembers. Implicit memories are in your consciousness, and you can retrieve this information. For example, how to do math problems. Explicit memories are those in your subconscious. For example, the words to a song, poem, or phrase you learned some time ago that you recall quickly are in your explicit memory. We operate implicit and explicit memories without much thought about them. When we look at the whole picture of our body, our memories are embedded in body sensations, impulsive actions, feeling surges, and our perceptions. Based on our experiences, known and unknown, we are liable to act or say things we may not understand. IPNB gives a place to look for foundation and understanding. The practice of being curious about my body, memories, attachment, and actions allowed me to make changes in my energy system. Be gentle and curious about this topic. If it calls to you, take your time and get support. You can always come back to this when the time is right. This knowledge is power.

Personal Experience: Rewriting My Story

As I previously shared, trauma responses can hide in plain sight in your daily life. The key is to stay curious, learn to recognize trauma responses, and use the tools you'll be learning about to help you heal. Here's an example of how I recognized a trauma response while at work and took the time to rewrite my story.

As a manager in an organization, I always had meetings on my calendar. One day, a meeting was on my calendar without a description. I asked the secretary about the meeting to see if she had additional information.

The secretary did not have additional information about the meeting. I began to physically not feel well. I was queasy. I had an uneasy feeling about the unknown meeting. I became moody, cranky, and unsettled about this mystery. I walked into the meeting room; everything for the presentation of the meeting was still being set up. I vented when I entered, seeing the meeting was not ready to start. It was about the lack of efficiency and inconvenience of my time. I was still in the dark about who called the meeting and why. I muttered under my breath about it not being on time.

When my coworker and friend heard me mutter that the presentation was not set up, she asked me, "What will you say yes to today, Lisa, because you are not saying yes to this meeting?" Moody, cranky, and unsettled, I sat down to wait for the meeting to start. I journaled to get insight into what was going on with me. I could not stop myself from being disgruntled. I wanted to change the way I felt, and I could not. I found out in my writing that my feeling of "unknown" or "doom" was a trauma response for me. At the time, I could not remember what had caused the memory in my body, I could not identify what had caused the discomfort. Later, I discovered my feelings were based on my very early upcoming. I lived in the home with several primary caregivers but without one central parent figure. The sense of not knowing was one that was lodged in my energy system. Not knowing what was going to happen at any given time must have felt unsafe. That same feeling is what I had at work that day.

That day at work, I rewrote my own story. "Although I did not know what would occur in this meeting, I am more than capable of doing my job. I am knowledgeable and can make decisions. If I need help, I can ask for it." My energy immediately shifted; the feeling of dread was gone! Later, I discovered my role in the meeting was as the decision-maker of what was being presented.

Trauma responses can be sounds, smells, touches, pictures, or anything that sparks the experience. They can even come in the form of joy or laughter. The thing to take away is that the body's response shapes how the body and brain work together. The body and brain are so magnificent in protecting us that we can continue to live our lives and not even realize harm has affected us.

Chapter Summary

In chapter 1, you become familiar with the truth about the trauma that lives in the body and how it can manifest in various forms. The body holds the stories of your life. Healing trauma requires the ability to notice and see it. This chapter shares the science of trauma and the interpersonal neurobiology of our body's work. Memories in our conscious and subconscious are like rivers running through us that can be invisible. This chapter included examples of how trauma shows up in everyday life through early childhood experiences, addiction, and various life challenges. The journal reflection and real-life experiences brought context to the learning and allowed you to participate at the beginning of your discovery.

RECOGNIZING TRAUMA IN THE BODY

Through our learning in chapter 1, you now have a better awareness of where trauma comes from (sources of trauma) and why and how it's stored in our body. The next step in this process is to apply that knowledge to your body. Because our individual experiences may differ widely and because each body will store trauma differently as a result, the way to recognize trauma in your own body is to start by getting to know your body and learning to quiet your body so you can hear what it's trying to communicate with you.

Every person is different, so there is no exact formula or recipe, but there are some tried-and-true exercises to try. This chapter will introduce you to many of the exercises I've found helpful throughout my healing journey.

To begin, reflect on these questions to get in touch with your body. Jot down your thoughts in your journal.

- What does your body enjoy the most?
- How do you relax your mind?
- Think about your hands and feet. What is their happiest place?
- If your arms could talk, what would they say to you?
- How do you pamper your body?
- Do you love your body?
- If you were to think of one step to get to know your body, what would it be?
- What part of your body needs the most love?
- If you have experienced harmful things to your body, have you provided care for your healing, body, mind, and soul?
- What does meditation mean to you?
- Are you open to trying meditation?
- Are you open to trying walking meditations?
- Are you open to trying dancing as a meditation?
- What do you do to calm your body, mind, and spirit?
- What brings you joy? What sensations does joy feel like in your body? Do you have joy in your life today?
- Make a list of joyful things in your life.

Think about your answers and consider the best way for you to connect to your body.

Need an easy way to get started with connecting your body and mind? Try taking a walk while using all your senses to fully take in your surroundings. Walk casually, clearing your mind and enjoying everything you witness. Another form of connection is music; listening to calming music or inspirational talks can soothe the soul. Imagine listening to music you love; you can easily be transported to another world.

Guided meditations are a great source of morning or evening quiet time. Guided meditations give focus and set a calm tone for your thoughts throughout the day. I have even listened to meditation content on the way to work. Focusing on the message, soft music, and soothing tones slows my heart rate and provides a calm and peaceful drive.

The critical thing to remember about whatever first steps you take is not to put pressure on yourself. This is a healing *journey*. It is not intended to be one that is harsh and oppressive. It is the opposite; it is intended to bring peace, heighten the senses, and heal the soul. Everything you try is fine; if you stop doing it for a period, that is fine too. There is no right or wrong thing to do or way to do it. What is important is that you keep experimenting and doing things that call you or somehow spark your interest. Be curious and invite in what the universe offers to you for your healing. Whatever inspires you, try it. The clear objective is to spend quiet time with yourself without negativity. Work toward a positive. You may realize the array of negative thoughts traveling through your mind. These thoughts are not part of you. Thoughts of love belong to you; anything else can be dismissed. To begin, try committing to three to five minutes of quiet time daily. What you will find if you continue to reach for it is peace.

Commit to taking action to calm your body. The following resource guide is provided to assist you in choosing and committing to actions for body awareness.

What to Look For in Your Body

We have discussed trauma living in the body and getting to know the body to remove the sore spots that are no longer needed. It is essential to understand at the body level what that may look like in your life. The following graphic is from Yoder's Strategies for Trauma Awareness and Resilience (STAR), which is a model written to identify and heal trauma and shows a representation of trauma called the Trauma Experience.

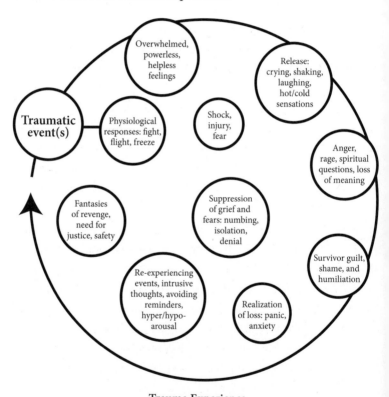

Trauma Experience
Referenced from Carolyn Yoder and
the STAR Team at Eastern Mennonite University

Look at the graphic and remember that the body responds to an event. The physical reaction is the bubbles inside the circle. Any of those responses could occur, or none may be a response. Trauma responses do not follow rules. One of the most puzzling things about trauma is that it is different for each person. One person may respond with anger or rage, while another may respond with powerlessness. We must start with the body and get to know it well so we can understand what is going on for us individually. The body has a connection to our subconscious and conscious selves. Learning how our bodies process harmful experiences will assist us in uncovering what may be hidden.

Look at the following cycles of violence graphic. It depicts the cycle of trauma responses that may occur in our bodies. An experience or event could activate an internal reaction or an external reaction, which are each represented in this graphic as acting in and acting out. Each response has the ability to change from an internal reaction to an external reaction. This process has the ability to move from one cycle to another, an infinity sign or continuous movement. This can be an ongoing cycle without any conscious awareness.

It is possible to experience harm and react to the past in an endless cycle. This cycle is what I felt as I responded to life and its challenges. I had a low motor running at all times. The cycle of trauma can mirror life. The words in the center of the circles can be the result of trauma experiences. These experiences are manifestations of harm. The harm is transformed and may resemble the examples provided. For example, working many hours a week and not caring for your health, diet, and rest is harmful. The words in the center represent the results of self-neglect. Again, these are not rules; other things may be true for you.

Powerless, helpless feelings

Shock, injury, fear, denial

Trembling, crying, heat, cold

Suppression of grief and fears

Anger, rage, spiritual questions, loss of meaning

Physiological responses: fight, flight, freeze

Depression

Workaholism

Silence, constricted emotions

Internalized oppression

Survivor guilt, shame, and humiliation

Traumatic event(s); acts of violence

Physical ailments

Self-abuse, addictions, intergenerational trauma

Suicide

Learned helplessness, fatalism

Realization of loss: panic, anxiety

Re-experiencing events, intrusive thoughts, avoiding reminders, hyper/hypo-arousal

Fantasies of revenge, need for justice, safety

Seeing self/group as victims, embracing "us" vs. "them" identity

Bullying

Attacking in the name of self-defense, justice, or honor

Creating and sustaining unjust structure and system

Experiencing unmet needs for safety and justice: shame, humiliation, fear

Sexual harm

Blaming others

Lawlessness

Domestic violence

Responding to social and cultural pressures, pride

Repetitive violence/war

Child abuse

Developing good vs. evil narrative

Dehumanizing the "other"

Deciding to pursue own needs, even at expense of others

Viewing violence as redemptive

Cycles of Violence
Referenced from Carolyn Yoder and
the STAR Team at Eastern Mennonite University

Past harms can live dormant under the surface of your body until an event awakens them. A past harm could involve the way you think about others or yourself. It could be the way you respond to others, institutions, or authority. Think of the analogy that if something is turned up to maximum volume, it is too high to listen to and is out of sync. These too-loud events live within your energy system. They are too high to work for you and cause your body and responses to be out of sync.

Journal Reflection: Cycles of Violence

Use the prompts below to capture your reflections about the previous section in your journal.

- Think about your life. Describe what you recognize in the bubbles on the outside of the circles in the cycles of violence graphic.
- What can you add to it?
- Draw how you experience responses to stress in your life.
- Describe what you recognize about the red letters in this graphic from your life.

IPNB Tools

In my year-long study, I picked up some valuable tools that have served me well. A couple of tools that helped me the most in IPNB were attunement and coregulation sharing practices.

Attunement

Attunement is the attribute of being present when someone is struggling through a trauma response. When I found out that I identified with multiple attachments, I did not feel good. My belly hurt, and I felt like my head was fuzzy. My partner in the workshop offered attunement; he was present with me and supported me until I felt better. Often, when a person has a trauma response, others are quick to want to fix the feeling by criticizing, judging, minimizing, dismissing, comparing, fact-finding, problem-solving, cheerleading, or dismissing. These actions do not help someone best handle a response to trauma. Attunement is the gentle and caring nature of being there with another human being. It could look like soft verbal assurances, soft gazes, or verbal acknowledgment such as, "I hear you," "Sorry that happened," "You did not deserve that," or appropriate outrage like, "What?!" Attunement also encompasses nonword sounds of encouragement and silence with comfort. Attunement is a tool to have available when processing trauma. It helped me regulate my body.

Coregulation Sharing

The coregulation sharing exercise involves processing something you experienced that did not feel good to you. It could be a disagreement, a conversation that did not go well, or a brief interchange that was not pleasant.

This activity requires two people. Each will take turns sharing their experience. The first step is to sit near your partner. Each person will take a turn to share about their experience. As each person shares about the situation, they focus on where in their body they feel a sensation and put their hand on that part of their body. The partner mirrors the action by putting their hand on their body in the same place. The listening partner practices attunement as they listen to their partner. The coregulation sharing helps process challenging situations and utilizes attunement as support.

When it was time to pair up, everyone in the class had a partner, and there was no one left for me to partner with. The instructor volunteered to work with me. I originally doubted the exercise, but then I was partnered with the teacher. I thought on my feet quickly about a situation I had worked through. I knew there would be no response to sharing it because I already had done the work to process it independently. I sat near the instructor—we were to sit close, not touching—and I started with my challenge from work involving the mystery meeting. I suddenly felt a sensation in my chest while sharing and put my hand on my chest. The instructor mirrored my actions, and I finished telling my story. After I shared, I was dumbfounded—the body sensation was gone. The sharing with attunement worked. Coregulation sharing with another attuned person was a powerful experience and support for my body.

How Else Can We See Trauma?

Other examples of what trauma can look like in your life come from the vast field of trauma practitioners. You can experience any of the feelings in the following list.

- Helplessness or pointlessness
- Feeling constantly behind
- On the watch for something to happen
- Not creative

- Anger; violent issues
- Self-deprivation as a way to self-worth
- Difficulty working, hard work
- Making something bigger than it needs to be, ignoring something that requires attention
- Physical problems, constant exhaustion
- Limited attention span
- Physically, emotionally, and mentally unavailable
- Negative self-talk
- Numbing out; shutting down
- Being a victim
- Guilt
- Fear
- No self-esteem
- Cycles of panic
- Self-hatred, including culture or heritage
- Lack of empathy
- Addictions
- Egocentric
- Learned helplessness
- Unhealthy friendships/relationships

Cyndi Dale—internationally renowned author, speaker, healer, and business consultant—discusses trauma experiences as caused by forces that can be positive or negative. The forces that do not work with our bodies can affect us physically and carry subtle charges that can negatively impact us. In her book *Energy Healing for Stress and Chronic Illness*, she states that energies can be affected in a variety of ways like attachment and holds, aches, pain, addictive tendencies, relationship desires or conflict, lies, hopes, dreams, feelings, thoughts, judgments, memories, and unwanted energy.

Looking at even a small amount of the available information about trauma, it is a wonder that some of us are unsure of what steps to take. Regardless of what direction is best for you, the first step is connecting with your body so you can discern what is happening. You can unearth and discard your life's sore places or responses by first connecting to your body.

The Three Levels of Healing

When we look at healing trauma, we can approach it in a three-level process:

- **Level 1: Body Sensations**—Tuning in to where and how trauma is stored in the body.

- **Level 2: Mind Patterns**—Bringing awareness to how our thoughts and behaviors are impacted by unhealed trauma.

- **Level 3: Reflective Tools for Positive Reconnection of the Body, Mind, and Spirit**—This is where we bring it all together.

This chapter covers the first step, which is Level 1 of the healing process, as shown in the following graphic.

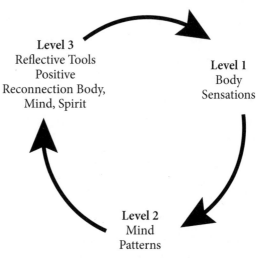

The Three Levels of Healing

By noticing when your body goes into a response cycle, you can be curious about the feelings surrounding what is going on in the moment and begin to walk toward healing that particular physical, mental, and spiritual feeling. Seeing what is going on in the body is the foundational step for healing.

Level 1 helps us understand how our body responds to trauma, how to identify those responses, and how to use tools for healing the body, mind, and spirit.

After acknowledging and connecting with your body, the next step is Level 2, which interrupts subconscious belief patterns in your thinking. Acknowledgment of trauma in the body makes space to witness your belief system. In Level 2, you will examine beliefs through your everyday experiences of life. Your belief system is closely associated with body functions. What you believe can be based on conscious or subconscious beliefs. You will become curious about your feelings and daily interactions, allowing you to take steps to uncover past harms and discover strengths. The trauma experiences you remember or do not remember can be identified and resolved through simple-to-use reflection tools in Level 2.

To hold on to our learning and reflections, Level 3 will help you break free and pave new roads into your body, mind, and spirit. By creating new healing pathways, the body and mind make space for the spirit. Paving a new road is breaking free from trauma, and it works best when there is a community of support. In Level 3, we will identify what kind of support fits you best physically, emotionally, and spiritually. This step integrates body, mind, and spirit tools to build the Breaking Free Cycle. This cycle includes the useful tools discovered at each level and combines them into a pathway one can follow and review when changes need to occur. This level also provides assistance, suggestions for support, and guidelines to sustain new ways of living as you continue to experience more positive energy.

With pathways moving forward, you can chart your process with Level 1. Use the reflection prompts in this chapter to assess where you are in Level 1 before moving to the next level—you'll experience the greatest results from this work when you are diligent about working through the steps mindfully. Be kind and gentle with yourself. If you find yourself challenged, find a buddy to work with and encourage each other. Resources for self-care can be found at the end of each chapter; you can locate a complete listing of the resources in the Wellness Tool Kit at the end of the book to make it easy to return to these exercises in the future.

In the next chapter, we will connect the mind and body.

Self-Care Tools and Exercises for Body Connection

At the end of each chapter going forward, you'll be guided through a series of self-care tools and exercises to help integrate the learning from the chapter and support your overall well-being. To stay connected to body, mind, and spirit, affirmations, meditations, and rituals are included, in addition to some daily self-care tools. We are building a practice that will support healing. The chapters build on each other, and the affirmations, meditations, and ritual experiences that follow will assist you in staying connected. The intention is to strengthen the body, mind, and spirit along the way. The expectation by the middle of the book is that you will have worked toward making the affirmations, meditations, and rituals personalized and intimate, and by the end of the book, you'll be well on your way to having built supportive lifelong practices. These are guidelines to assist you on a path to healing.

The following tools are provided to get you started building your Wellness Tool Kit. Each chapter moving forward will provide you with additional tools and resources to continue experimenting with—add the ones you enjoy and find beneficial to your daily tool kit, and make sure to check with your doctor or healthcare provider if you have questions about any self-care tools provided in the book.

Breathing: Focusing on the Breath, Slow Breathing

The following breathing patterns can provide relief while working through trauma.

Box Breathing

Step 1: Breathe in, counting to four slowly. Feel the air enter your lungs.

Step 2: Hold your breath for four seconds. Try to avoid inhaling or exhaling for four seconds.

Step 3: Slowly exhale through your mouth for four seconds.

Step 4: Repeat steps 1 to 3 until you feel recentered.

Pursed Lip Breathing

You slowly inhale through your nose and gently exhale through pursed lips.

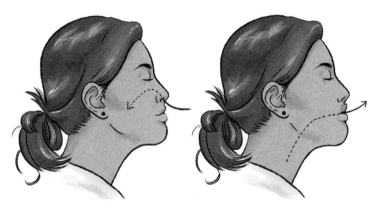

Pursed Lip Breathing

4-7-8 Breathing

The 4-7-8 technique involves inhaling for four seconds, holding your breath for seven seconds, and exhaling for eight seconds.

Alternate Nostril Breathing

Slowly breathe in and out through one nostril while keeping the other one closed with your fingers. Rotate to the other nostril and do the same.

Alternate Nostril Breathing

Visualization

Imagine yourself in a place that brings you peace and calm (beach, waterfall, mountains, floating). To help, you can also look at images or videos or listen to audio of these calming places, animals, or other nature sounds.

Music

Listen to music that brings joy.

Binaural Beats

These are sound recordings that use frequencies that the brain interprets as one. This one tone can assist in helping your body relax.

Inspirational Reading

Read a book with a positive message and focus for the day.

Nature

Spend time out in nature, soaking it up, exploring with all your senses.

Sleep

Do you know there are patterns to how we sleep (light sleep, deep sleep, and vivid dreaming)? Sleeping is crucial because during the wee hours of the night and early morning, your body conserves and restores energy, repairs and recovers, and experiences brain maintenance. If your relationship with sleep is a challenge, it may be a help to reflect on the underlying issues. Use your journal to reflect on the following questions.

- How much healthy sleep do you get each night? How do you know?
- Have you ever examined your sleeping patterns?
- What actions can you take to ensure you are sleeping well each night?
- What is your attainable sleep goal for the next six months?

Suggestions for supporting healthy sleeping habits include going to sleep at a consistent time, minimizing electronics and screen time before bed, avoiding large meals a few hours prior to sleep, and limiting caffeine intake in the evening. Regular exercise also contributes to good sleeping habits.

Apps for sleep tracking can assist in getting a picture of your sleep needs and with collecting information to inform your goals moving forward. I have been using a sleep app for some time to assist me with monitoring my sleep quality. Some apps are free, while others ask for a small fee.

Exercise

Do you exercise regularly? Movement is necessary to bring balance and health into our lives. The point of exercise is to get movement into your regular lifestyle. The comment I hear the most about exercise is that time is a factor. If your relationship with exercise is challenging, this is a starting place to reflect on the underlying issues.

- How much movement do you get in your day-to-day life that is not organized exercise?
- What do you enjoy most about the ways you use movement in your life?
- Is there a problem fitting movement into your life? Where in your body do you feel a sensation when you think about movement if it is an issue for you?
- If you exercise regularly, what do you do and are you open to trying other forms of exercise?
- What is your attainable movement goal for the next six months?

Let's reframe the relationship with movement and take steps to include regular movement in your life. Here are some low-key movement ideas to get you started:

- Walking in nature
- Dancing: ecstatic dance, free dance, dance party, dance classes
- Biking: even electronic bikes give support and get you moving
- Hiking: short hikes, city hikes, park hikes
- Yoga: in person or online
- Low-impact exercises

No matter how you choose to move, be kind to yourself. This is about care.

Food Choices

Do you monitor your food choices? Certain foods are not necessarily good for our energy. Consuming foods that are mostly made well makes a difference in how we feel. Take some time to reflect on what you are eating and whether it is yielding the feeling you desire. If your relationship with food is one that is a challenge, a great place to start is to reflect on any underlying issues related to food. Take this time to reflect in your journal and see what will work to help you be your very best.

- Do you eat a well-balanced diet that makes your body feel good?
- What foods work well for your body?
- Have you examined what works for your body and what does not?
- How do you know if you are eating what your body needs?

Here are some resources to take a deeper look at your relationship with your body and food:

- Meditations on food as energy. Oprah Winfrey and Deepak Chopra have a twenty-one-day meditation series called "Getting Unstuck: Creating a Limitless Life" that helped me a lot. I yo-yo with weight gain and this meditation assisted me with changing the way I thought about energy and food.
- Examine what works in other countries; widen your scope.
- Keep it simple and increase your water intake.
- Drink clean, filtered water.
- Look at the foods you eat and learn about their properties and benefits.

Again, remember to be kind to yourself while examining your food habits. This exercise is about care, not judgment.

Affirmations

Affirmations are positive thoughts showered on the body, mind, and spirit. These words assist the mind in providing a high vibration to the body. When you start your day, take a deep breath in through your nose and out through your mouth before reading the affirmation to yourself out loud. This starts your day with positive phrases and high vibrations. Each day upon awakening, breathe in the goodness of life through positive affirmations. By the end of this book, you will have created affirmations and morning practices that are best for your body, mind, and spirit.

While I encourage you to write your own affirmations, here are a few to get you started:

I am light and goodness.
My body and mind work in the betterment of my life.
I am worthy of love and compassion.
I have love and compassion for myself.
As I seek truth, I will be led to goodness.

Meditation

If you are just beginning to sit quietly, set a timer and start at three, five, or ten minutes. Pick a time you are comfortable sitting. Do not let your mind tell you that you are not able to sit in silence for whatever reason. When the thoughts come to defeat your intention, push them away and proceed. These defeating thoughts are part of the trauma protection and part of the un-healed mind that interferes with healing. Start now to notice its messages and gently push them away. You can simply state *not today* or *not now*.

Find a quiet place where you are comfortable and feel safe. Set-tle yourself where you are sitting. You can lie down if that is com-fortable. Take a deep breath in. Focus your energy and thoughts on your body and how you're breathing. If your breath is rapid, slow yourself down.

Repeat in your mind:

I am safe. I am safe. I am safe.

Imagine you are in your favorite place (beach, mountains, porch, a swing, etc.). Picture the setting in your mind's eye. Look at every aspect of the setting. If your mind tells you that you cannot see it, just pretend you can. Tap into your inner child of wonder. Look around you and find a place to be comfortable. If you are struggling to see your special place, pick a place that brings you joy and tell yourself you are there enjoying the surroundings.

Take a deep breath in and slowly blow it out.

If your mind is wandering, bring it back. If your mind continues to wander, begin to count backward from ten to one slowly.

Continue to take deep breaths in and out.
Continue to take deep breaths in and out.
Continue to take deep breaths in and out.
Continue to take deep breaths in and out.
Continue to take deep breaths in and out.

Breathe slowly until the timer goes off. Thank your body, wiggle your finger and limbs, and slowly open your eyes.

Continue to build this practice until you can feel your body sink into relaxation. Do not be discouraged if it does not happen right away. It takes time to nurture your body. If sitting independently is too much, begin with guided meditations starting at one minute and increase the time as needed. The important part is to start.

Rituals

The rituals in each chapter are designed to assist you in developing positive ways to connect to yourself and the universe. It is easy for us to simply jump out of bed and rush to start our day. Having committed rituals allows us regular pauses to stop, take a breath, have a gentle laugh, or walk outside and end our day with a positive wrap-up to create a culture of love for ourselves. This intentional daily space is missing for many people. The intention is that by the end of the book, you will have developed and cultivated your own way of pausing the busyness of the world to take time for yourself.

Morning

When you open your eyes from slumber, take a deep breath in and slowly blow it out. Take a moment of gratitude before you do anything else like grab your phone. Center yourself in gratitude. The gratitude can be as simple as a thank-you. Take another deep breath in and slowly blow it out. Have a great day.

Gratitude Ideas

Write a list of gratitudes to use in your morning awakening. Here are a couple of ideas to get you started: *I'm grateful for this bed. I am grateful for my arms, legs, eyes, and the ability to breathe.*

Noon

Around noon, stop and take a breath. It does not matter what is going on in your life. When you see it is midday, stop and breathe in a positive thought. You are important and worth this brief pause. Think about something that brings you joy (a pet, a fun moment, a loved one, a favorite memory).

Evening

In the evening, before dinner or at bedtime, take a moment to breathe in a positive moment by reading something inspirational. This will only take a minute or two. Read an inspirational quote or daily reader with positive messages. Here are a few to start with. Continue to add to this list as you find new ones.

> *Every day has a jewel of love;*
> *we must open our eyes to see it.*

*Love is the blanket of care the universe gives
us. I want more and more of the blanket and
less and less of what lives outside of it.*

*The earth is ever yearning for me to sit and lie
with it. The days I cherish are the ones when
we can spend hours in joyful kinship.*

*I know I am at peace when the world and all its
activity stands still and I am one with stillness of my
body, mind, and spirit. My body feels like it's sus-
pended in a fluffy cloud without a worry in the world.*

———————

The previous tools are suggested based on personal experience. I have found success with guided meditation, morning inspiration reading, and light exercise as an entry point to getting to know my body and thinking process.

Commit to trying something to connect with your body. If you have experienced a violation of your body, this work may require additional professional support. This resource is not a substitute for professional mental health or medical assistance. Do not be discouraged; take one step at a time and commit to one thing.

In your journal, describe what you will commit to trying and date it.

Journal Reflection: Chapter Insights

Gather your journal for the beginning of your reflection and learning journey. Now that we've taken a deep dive into the material for this chapter, it's time to reflect on what you learned, insights you gained along the way, and how you're experiencing the journey thus far. You'll have an opportunity to do this throughout and at the end of each chapter in the book. These reflection exercises are designed to provide you with time to consider how you feel and think about how you want to move forward as more tools are introduced to support your new knowledge in each chapter.

Use the following prompts to reflect on your body connection from this chapter in your journal. The following guiding questions are provided to assist you in this reflection process.

- Describe places in your life that bring up feelings when you think about them.
- Describe in your body whether, where, and how you feel discomfort in your day-to-day living.
- Describe your biggest takeaway from the chapter.
- Create a goal for getting in touch with your body.
- Describe your current self-care habits.

Chapter Summary

Chapter 2 is a launching pad for your healing journey. In this chapter, you try on the information from the previous chapter and start using your new learning as you go. The identification of trauma in one's body and life depend on one's relationship with the body. This chapter begins by building a bridge to body self-awareness. The chapter starts with reflective thinking and writing about one's relationship with one's body. It then provides information to enhance your understanding of what happens in the body when a trauma occurs. This chapter highlights Caroline Yoder's 2001 STAR model, which includes two graphics that illustrate what can happen when a trauma occurs. The STAR cycles of violence model (graphic 1) depicts how trauma can manifest and keep going. The STAR breaking free building resilience model (graphic 2) suggests breaking free from trauma through acknowledgment and reconnection with self. This chapter also introduces the three healing levels: Level 1, Body Sensations; Level 2, Mind Patterns; and Level 3, Reflective Tools Positive Reconnection Body, Mind, and Spirit (graphic 3).

This chapter connects to all you have learned and processed to support the work with Level 1, Body Sensations. Journal reflections in this chapter connect your thinking and feelings about how trauma can show up in your life. By incorporating IPNB tools to nurture yourself, your path has begun. The chapter closes with thoughtful reflections, a self-care library to choose from, and suggestions to begin daily practices of affirmations, meditation, and rituals to ground your road to healing.

CHAPTER THREE
HOW TRAUMA SHOWS UP

The body is an amazing creation! It protects us and keeps us safe even when we do not realize it. Many people have experienced some form of trauma in their lives; it is the human experience. The problem with harmful experiences is that most people think it is not a big deal. Many of us want to move on and put accidents or harmful events in the past. We do not live in a culture that normalizes hearing about feelings and working through them. Most of us think that whatever has happened is not a big deal, therefore, we are fine. Dismissing harmful experiences causally is a form of ignoring trauma responses. It is a way to keep moving by not stopping and dealing with the challenge. Ignoring does not work with trauma in the long run. Our bodies are our friends and we have a responsibility to listen to our bodies or wait for our bodies to get our attention.

To build on the information from the last chapter, it is necessary to connect our body awareness with our thinking. The body can send very subtle messages, which can be difficult to detect if you're not paying attention. If you have taken steps toward getting to know your body from chapters 1 and 2, you may have made some impressions about your body.

As I previously shared, when I first started learning about trauma, I had not been looking for my own healing; I did not believe I had lived through traumatic experiences before learning the truth about trauma. The stark reality was revealed when my body began to respond to stressful situations. Chapters 1 and 2 laid the foundation of getting you and your body to the point of restful peace. When peace occurs, your mind can experience calm without effort. Calm without effort is a quiet mind that does not include running thoughts. Before being able to articulate what happened in my life, I began to seek more and more peacefulness by paying attention to my body's messages.

For example, after my divorce in my late twenties, I worked as a teacher's aide in a private school. The job required me to take directions from my supervisor, the teacher in charge of the classroom. The school served students who struggled with mental and emotional health, so the job was more than paperwork; it took emotional calmness and environmental awareness to keep everyone safe. One day, the teacher gave me directions during class, and suddenly, I felt like I was twelve years old and wanted to fight and argue with the teacher about her directions. These emotions happened in my body and flooded me so quickly that I was overwhelmed with anger. I excused myself and went to the bathroom and began journaling. What came out of my writing is that I was responding to how my father, at times, berated me. I do not know what specifically triggered my body to remember those childhood experiences. As an adult, I stood in the bathroom and talked myself back into my body. *I am not twelve, and she is not my dad. I am not twelve, and she is not my dad. I am not twelve, and she is not my dad.* I caught my breath, and I became ready to take her direction.

At that time, I did not question the feeling or try to understand what happened. If I argued with my boss, I would not have a job, so I worked around my feelings. Understanding your body and its subtle responses is the foundation of trauma healing work. Throughout my healing journey, the information I received from my body was so subtle that originally I thought it came from my thoughts and desires. Sometimes, feelings were positive, and other times, they were not. A clue to being unbalanced would present itself when I struggled. I was used to factual feelings; whatever happened should be solved outside of me. The fact that my body was protecting me and I was responding to something that was not real had not occurred to me. Separating who I was from my experiences was something that took intentional action, and that is what this book is about.

When instances of remembering past harm occur, I believe most of us move on and discount the feelings in the moment. These memories are rooted in something deeper. Something deeper is what will be examined closely in this chapter. Use the following reflection to see where you are in your body response exploration.

Journal Reflection: Body Connection

Use the prompts below to capture your reflections about the previous section in your journal. These guiding questions are provided to assist you in this reflection process.

- What actions have you taken to get to know your body?
- What have you noticed about your body and its responses?

Body exploration is vital to move to the next step. In my case, I was very disconnected from my body. I was not fluent with emotions and came from a culture of getting the job done, whatever it takes—we did not stop to feel things along the way. It was not any one thing that people said or did that gave me this impression; it was the culture of my surroundings. My parents were really hard workers. Both came from humble beginnings, and getting things done was how success happened. As I began to pay attention to my body and its sensations, I noticed a few things. For example, I ate for comfort. I was often not hungry, and I ate anyway. One of the most fascinating times of awareness in this area was after I got up from eating dinner. My stomach would growl in hunger. I thought this was very strange. I just got up from the dinner table. I could not be hungry. But I had been struggling with issues at work. I put the two things together and could see my body wanted food for comfort, but my mind knew better. The habit of eating for comfort started to decrease when I paid attention to the urges from my body and mind.

I told myself I would be alright and did not need to eat to feel better. Those impulses of eating for comfort decreased under emotional strain.

Remember that a trauma response can be a sound, smell, touch, picture, or anything that sparks the experience. It can be joy or laughter too. By knowing your body, you can be curious about the response and look deeper to heal it.

Having knowledge about the forms of trauma will assist you in being able to put experiences in the proper context.

Recognizing Trauma Sources

In the previous chapters, trauma was discussed in various ways. This section will review the sources of trauma to assist you in recognizing it. We will examine how you picked up these long-lasting experiences and did not notice their existence.

Acute Trauma

Trauma can stem from something that happened one time or from something that is ongoing and keeps happening. You may have heard of acute trauma. It is a one-time isolated traumatic event. Post traumatic stress disorder occurs when people experience shocking, life-threatening events. This term was coined by American psychiatrists after examining soldiers who returned from World War II in 1945. Trauma can be caused by a natural event or by interactions with people. We could experience something by ourselves or with a group.

Secondary or Vicarious Trauma

One can also experience trauma by witnessing the struggle of other people, which is called secondary or vicarious trauma.

First responders witness the struggle of others in their day-to-day interactions. It takes its toll on all human beings and animals. Think about something you have seen that did not sit right with you. The first thing you felt was in your body. Maybe you got a wave of anger, or you wanted to move to another location. Perhaps you tried to take over the situation and lead others to safety. Whatever happened, an instinct took over. This instinct is an example of a trauma response. It takes over very quickly. The feelings are like a wave over your body. It can be very subtle or significantly over the top. You may jump into action or become very silent.

If you have experienced someone jumping into a pool and breaking their neck, you may always see pool diving as a threat. You may avoid it, and you will tell yourself it is your choice, when in reality, it is not. When your body has experienced a harmful experience, part of your nervous system remembers it, and that memory becomes a warning sign. Is it harmful that your body remembers? No, it is not. The trauma response becomes a problem when you are making decisions, having feelings, and not living how you would like because of the reactions. The incidents that continue to bring you discord are the ones we want to remove and then heal the space it once held. Incidents are remembered in your energy system even if you do not remember them explicitly.

Media today is full of violent content of people being killed or hurt physically and emotionally. War scenes, children and families in cages, and stories of people being strangled have been shown on our news channels increasingly in the last few years. How can any of us not experience some reaction to these unsettling and graphic images? Digesting these images affects our body, mind, and soul. Over some time, we can become desensitized to disturbing images, words, and content. This lack of connectedness affects us profoundly, and when we need to be there for ourselves or others, we may miss the opportunity. Let's face it: if something is horrible and sad, it is just that, and the best thing to do is to feel our feelings and let them burn off. When I was growing up, I learned to "suck it up" and not acknowledge my feelings. The message I received was to not feel my feelings and just keep moving. This action left a mark on my energy centers and distorted how I processed living day to day.

Historical Trauma

Historical trauma describes the continuous psychological and emotional harm from historical events across generations. For example, slavery in the United States, the conflict between Catholics and Protestants in Northern Ireland or the conflict between different cultures in the Middle East. The removal and genocide of Native people from their lands across the Americas is another example of historical trauma; over eighty-two tribes were exterminated in the settlement of the United States. Native American researcher Maria Yellow Horse Brave Heart developed the Historical Trauma Training (1992–2003). Brave Heart was motivated to reduce the suffering of Indigenous people. She was influenced by the reality of the past, shaping the present, and the unconscious/preconscious thinking that lived in the people living on reservation communities. The researcher believed powerful memories lived in the bodies of Native people and brought a sense of unhealed grief and trauma to the broader tribal community. Historical trauma requires communities to acknowledge and address the legacy of trauma.

Today, Native populations continue to struggle with daily life since the settlement of the United States and the removal of Native Americans from their homelands. Their ancestors' cultures, lives, and ways of being were taken from them. I wish it were easy to fix, but it is not. Historical trauma of Native Americans lives in us all. As human beings, we are all responsible for harm caused to our community. In chapter 6, we will visit community wellness with complex healing topics.

There are many examples of historical trauma across different cultures in the United States and abroad. This trauma spans the enslavement of Africans, their descendants, those Europeans who enslaved people, and those Europeans who did not enslave others and their descendants. In my opinion, healing is one that takes a community approach. Like Native Americans, Africans who were kidnapped and brought to America lost their culture and assimilated to survive in the new land. This survival is one that passed down trauma and trauma-related ways of being.

An example of how this generational trauma still exists can be seen in my strong feelings to control my young Black sons in public. My sons are young Black men. Correction: my sons are young Black boys, not men. This subconscious word choice is a form of generational and historical trauma. Young Black boys are not Black men and should not be thrust into positions to equate them with manhood. This thought is often seen in public discourse about Black boys looking older than their age. The healing work for me continues in these areas of generational and historical trauma. Without understanding the connection to the generational trauma, I tried to maintain close control of my sons in public. They needed to stand still, be polite, take direction, and so on. My desire to control these young souls did not come from my experiences. My feelings, thoughts, and actions were based on harms from past generations. My actions mirrored being in a war-torn country or in a life-or-death situation. Yet, something in me felt like it was life or death, and it was not. Trauma leaks out no matter what the family structure or culture.

Don't forget what happened to Emmett Till would echo in my mind. Emmett Till was a young Black boy who was brutally murdered in the South for supposedly speaking to a white woman. His mutilated body was publicly viewed at his funeral in 1955 in Chicago. Why does this experience echo in my mind? I was not born in 1955 and I did not witness this incident. The trauma from this event lives on and has not been healed. This event, like many others, haunts our systems and our world. Historical trauma lives in the lives of all of us. Each of us holds a piece of humanity for one another.

Historical and generational trauma of slavery is in my family system. I needed to heal the harm of the past by reviewing issues as they came up, like the control of my sons in public, to unlearn the historical trauma that lived in my body. *Post Traumatic Slave Syndrome* by Joy DeGruy notes that what was needed to survive enslavement is not what is needed today. When we continue to live in these past stories, it harms our body, mind, and spirit. This trauma is also true for those with European ancestry, or any other culture, whether their ancestors were enslavers, fought against enslavers, or lived through war and genocide. A soul's sickness lives in the body and must be reconciled to find peace. Healing work is our community working together.

There is no competition for who was harmed most in the United States or abroad. What is important is that many cultures were harmed throughout the world, more than what we learned in high school history class. Chinese Americans experienced hardship, isolation, and oppression in the United States. Some Chinese Americans lost touch with family members because of the nomadic lifestyle needed for their culture's survival and maintenance. Latin countries underwent colonialist overtaking in the fifteenth and sixteenth centuries before the Roman Catholic Church became a leading power in their culture and life. Today, many cultures and identities are misunderstood and mistreated.

I am sharing with you this information because each of these harms is still mostly unhealed for us as a community. As a society, we can only talk about them briefly and then move on. Those who come from the Jewish Holocaust or the forty-one genocides from around the world will have to examine their origins and ancestors. We all have work to do in this area.

I did. I needed to heal the harm that was showing up in my body through controlling parenting, fear of being attacked and harmed, fear for my children's lives, and lack of trust. These things lived in me; if you had asked me about them before my healing work, I would have told you I was simply a careful and protective mom.

I have witnessed others living in past trauma in their day-to-day lives. For example, I have heard stories like, "Grandma lived during the Depression." As a result, she stashed money in different banks in different towns and hid money in the mattresses, fearing the banks would collapse. Her family hoarded food for fear of being hungry. She had to make provisions to save everything in case of another financial collapse.

My family were farmers who worked in the summer to stock up for winter. I have repeatedly heard stories about how other families would come to my grandmother for food in the winter. The large family of ten worked hard in the summer, while others enjoyed not working. My grandmother would always share food with these people who came for help. In turn, the family's siblings keep food stocked in their home. Additional freezers are available to freeze food and keep provisions. As an adult, I found myself thinking that I had to do the same. It was what my family had done for generations. My spouse once asked me why I had to have so much food in the house. Our shelves were bursting—we had more food than we could eat. I did not have an answer, but when I looked back at my family's history and noted the food scarcity, I could see that it was passed down to me without my conscious acknowledgment. Some of these issues are spoken about within families, but most remain unspoken and exist under the surface.

By examining your ancestry and family system with curiosity, you can learn about what energy may carry harm in the form of historical trauma within your family. Harms may have occurred where you live or in your lineage. The most crucial thing in this section is to ask yourself, are you living it today? In some ways, you may bring the past into your daily life without even realizing it. Do you interact with someone who brings the past harm into your daily existence? If so, it is time to recalibrate and care for yourself and not go down the path that leads to more trauma. Trauma effects can be hidden in your family and cultural systems and the family and cultural systems of those in your life as well.

Cultural Trauma

Cultural trauma is the harm people experience because of their culture. Cultural and historical trauma can intersect. An example of cultural trauma is when culture is being erased (Native Americans and Jewish people in the Holocaust). The genocide of Jewish people in concentration camps is an example of a cultural trauma and historical trauma. The internment of Japanese Americans in the 1940s in the United States is cultural and historical trauma. The mistreatment of Muslim people after 9/11 in the United States is also cultural trauma. For some, this may be new information. When I visited the capitol in Washington DC to meet with legislators, an outpour of support in the form of sticky notes covered the office door of a Muslim representative who had just been removed from a committee. I found the display of support moving and wondered if the removal had been because of her culture. Cultural trauma can show up in many forms. For example, when my daughter was in college, she learned to wear hair wraps and other African clothing. Once, on her way home, she went into the bathroom at the airport and took off her hair wrap because of the hostility she was receiving from airport staff and fellow travelers. Culture makes our world unique, and when examining trauma, we must look in places we do not expect. If you turn your nose up at or look away quickly from those from other cultures, you are participating in some judgment. This judgment is one we want to curb. At this point, be open to acknowledging inhuman treatment, feelings, and conscious and subconscious actions. Doing this helps us love ourselves better.

Structural Trauma

Structural harm describes the political, economic, and social practices that continue to create oppression in societies. Many struggle to see this trauma. Because of the way colonialism works, many countries, including the United States, had morals, values, and tenets in place to uphold the intent of those who settled in this country. That means that things in our society are designed to work well for some and not others.

One example is the lack of medical care for people during the 2020 pandemic. During this time, some people were able to get medical attention while others were neglected. People of higher socioeconomic status were able to buy masks, water, and hand sanitizer in a timely manner, while those without resources had to make do with the information and resources available to them. This is structurally traumatic; the structures in place support those with wealth and power to receive the most care while those with limited resources receive little care. Growing up in poverty is a structural trauma, and it is one that is not addressed directly in our society. I have been in many learning opportunities where those who had tough upbringings in poverty fought against the cultural needs of others. It was the structural trauma coming forth, not that they did not want others to benefit. Structural trauma can be influenced by other factors like poverty, race, gender, or lack of healthcare.

Another example of structural trauma is the challenge of acquiring and maintaining mental healthcare—the struggle to keep and sustain services relies on insurance. Buying a home, getting a college education, or applying for a loan all have structural components. The systems of society and daily living can be harmful for some.

It is important to always gauge what trauma is pulling at you and keep in mind your experiences and the experiences of your ancestors as you undo what may be affecting your life today.

Participatory Trauma

Participatory trauma is experienced from playing a role when trauma occurs. Teachers experience participatory trauma when they may need to restrain a child, call social services when a child is hurt, or experience violence in the school setting. The role of police in society in the United States is fraught with participatory trauma.

Once, while I was in a grocery store, the manager and security of the store physically removed from the store a man who lived without a home. It was the saddest incident to witness. Four people held each limb and carried the man out of the store while he fought back. It was obvious he was unkempt and he did not look healthy. My heart was broken for both the man without a home who fought every step of the way and for the people who were removing him. Your heart has to break when you participate in such an overt action of removal. The key word again here is acknowledgment. We have to acknowledge how we feel in our bodies and that something has happened.

Dignity Violations

Dignity violations occur when a person is treated inhumanely. This trauma can be seen daily in the news, social media, and day-to-day conversations. Ignoring someone in public, bumping into people on the sidewalk as if you do not see them, and glaring mean looks at people are all dignity violations. The negativity that we share with others through a gesture, look, or words is so harmful. After moving to the Pacific Northwest, I stopped making eye contact with people in public because I would receive the most unwelcome exchanges back from people. I would receive more negative responses than positive ones, and although no words were exchanged, my body would feel the rejection of those who transferred those feelings consciously or subconsciously.

Whatever the cause, harm that occurs is perceived as serious, and our bodies respond to protect us. These experiences are all captured in the body. Although I may not seem to process the events that happen all around me each day, my body does, and that is where the ongoing processing of an event can color my personality and responses to life.

Think about the possibility of having an experience that you thought was behind you, yet it lives in your body as a reminder and protector. You may have experienced it by yourself or with a group of other people, and on the surface, it came to an end, but the alert to protect you from it in the future lingers in your body.

As shown in the cycles of violence graphic in chapter 2, one traumatic incident can hinder other life experiences; therefore, all of us have at some time experienced something that lingers. The indicator of a lingering effect is discovered by how we perceive new experiences. I noticed this lingering when I sought health more and more. I did not understand how or why I responded to feelings and emotions and life in general, and that curiosity led me to heal. Because of the complex nature of these trauma responses in our lives, it helps to know about the different kinds of traumas to help us navigate toward removing what is no longer needed.

Knowing about some of the traumas that could be part of your system will help you identify when your body is responding to them.

The Four Body Responses

If you are like me, you may be wondering what body responses look like in your life. Once you begin to get in touch with yourself, you'll start to notice feelings that will lead you to past experiences you can examine.

The body responds in fight, flight, fawn, or flock. If you are not familiar with these terms, they can seem unrelated. When the body senses danger, our nervous system takes over and responds in one of those categories:

- Fight: I will fight my way out.
- Flight: I need to get out of here.
- Fawn: I need you to like me.
- Flock: I need the comfort of others.

The rational brain sits down, and the emotional brain takes control. Think about that for a minute. Your rational thinking and reasoning take a seat, and your emotional thinking is calling the shots. When searching for trauma to heal, you are looking for the magic split-second moment when the emotional brain tries to take over your everyday life. It happens so fast that it is almost invisible. By getting to know the body, you become more and more alert, and you will become more capable at noticing when your rational brain sits down and your emotional brain takes over. When you notice these switches, it is a sign to start caring for yourself instead of responding to what has caused them. In our daily lives, we want to strive to live in the *window of tolerance*. The window of tolerance is the space where we are not overloaded or numbing out. It is our happy place for our body, mind, and spirit. The gift of knowing about trauma helps us maintain peace.

As my healing journey continued to evolve following that first impactful training session, a few significant movements catapulted me deeper into healing and well-being. I was introduced to a form of life coaching that highlighted body and mind awareness and introduced me to the inner workings of myself. Conscious Freedom Coaching opens learning by examining and transforming issues that interfere with happiness. The tools that showed me how to examine my subconscious were life changing. I found myself immobilized by the awareness and realization of feelings, ideas, and habits that lived in my subconscious. I felt a sense of awe when finding out things about myself. I could see and feel the healing. I was honored to be in the first cohort of Conscious Freedom coaches. I used all of what I learned to enhance my growth. The tools I learned here are also interwoven into this book.

Specifically, IPNB taught me that when trauma or harmful experiences occur, my body protects me and stores the experience in a space where I do not feel it. If anything comes near it, I could respond suddenly. This protection is my body's defense. My body has memories that are known and unknown based on social input that is integrated within me. A well-known axiom in the healing community states, what fires together wires together and survives together. This axiom says that when something comes close to an experience, it is called remembering. I learned that I am a result of my living experiences.

Much like a windblown tree on a cliff, my thoughts, ideas, and feelings have been molded by the winds in my life. When I heal old harm, the energy from that harm transforms into my body for good. I loved that. What I needed was the relationships around me to offer attunement. I needed attunement for my health and well-being. I did not develop alone, and I would not recover alone without healing relationships of support. In my recovery, relationships that included the qualities of attunement would benefit my growth.

How Trauma Can Affect You

Here are a few real-life examples of how trauma can affect you. When you read through these experiences, pay attention to how the trauma shows up in the responses for each person.

Car Accident Relived

Joe was in several serious car accidents when he was younger. He does not share his nervousness or fear about riding in cars. Yet, if he is not in control of driving, he overreacts at the slightest bump or sudden stop. He apologizes and laughs it off in the moment, but it is obvious his body is holding the memory of every car accident like it happened yesterday.

Violent Fighting

Carol was at a party with a group of people she knew and some she did not know. The party was at a neighbor's house. During the party the owners of the house got into a very heated argument and fight. Carol jumped up to run out of the house as she heard violent screaming and items breaking and being thrown around. As she jumped up to leave, her friend grabbed her hand and pulled her back down and looked at her sternly. Carol had never been around violence like this. The high-pitched screaming and fighting were terrifying and her heart was beating so fast. After some time, the couple came back into the room and sat down scratched up and bloody, and the party continued. Carol waited for quite some time to get back to the safety of her home. Now, anytime she hears high-pitched screaming or things being knocked about, her body travels back to that time and she is on alert to call for help.

Trusting Others

Incidents do not have to be huge to leave a mark on your energy centers. When I was a kid, I was painfully burned by a cigarette at an adult party. I was very young, about five years old. I remember it hurt a lot. I watched adults with cigarettes after that and learned I needed to watch out for myself. I realized that adults were not watching out for me, and I no longer trusted them to be careful with cigarettes. I was also not comforted or cared for after being burned. Comfort is kind and gentle and typically occurs when an incident like a cigarette burn happens to a child.

Hugging

When I was a new mother, one of my mentors asked me if I hugged my child after a disappointment. No, I stated plainly. You need to hug them and comfort them, my mentor told me. I began to do so because she told me to, not because it was natural to hug someone as a form of support and comfort. I did not grow up with comfort or hugs, leaving me a bit staunch and stiff in emotional situations. Before working on healing, I would proclaim, this is the way I am, but it is not. I did not have the experience of comfort or physical touch as a support. My spouse would often ask if I wanted a hug. The answer was always no or, "Why do you want to give me a hug?" My normal way of being becomes my default. Hugging me was like hugging a tree. I stood very rigid, and it felt like an invasion of my personal space, which I had to protect.

I share these life-lived nuances to spark curiosity in you to wonder about ways that do not serve you. Hugs are awesome, and I love them. How I was able to shift my thinking and actions came from paying attention to my body, thoughts, and actions, understanding where the idea of *I don't like hugs* came from, and resetting my system to serve me today.

I Am Alone

Other incidents happened in my childhood that reinforced the idea that I was required to watch out for myself and my own safety. Watching out for myself became a theme throughout my childhood and adult life. Growing up, watching out for myself was a protective shield. In adulthood, it has a bit of a different twist. If I am the only person I can count on, it makes for hard-to-manage and unhealthy, colored relationships with others who want to have a relationship with me. I can easily think that the people who care about me are not trustworthy. I never say these things, but I take action to make sure I am the one who has the final say. It is a spiritual axiom that my protection of myself pushes others away or attracts those who want to be cared for by others. I end up taking on others' problems and life challenges to keep myself safe. I seem to think I have poor luck in partnerships, when in reality, I am the driver of not trusting others. It took me some time to get to these conclusions; it did not happen overnight. My awareness began with noticing my body's reactions, thoughts, and actions.

Secondary Trauma

My supervisor once asked me to assist at an office that was in the midst of emotional fallout following a coworker's suicide. Many did not know the person well, but they were aware of that person's struggles, work-related bullying, and the oppressive practices against them because of their race and sexual identity. My job at the time was not to provide emotional support; I went to that office simply to be another person on site.

When I got to the location, many of the colleagues of the person who had died were angry and lashing out verbally at management. The support that was present did not know how to handle this anger. The atmosphere was chaotic, and people were expressing grief through rage. It felt sad and out of control. I suddenly was filled with sadness. It was almost like the situation was happening to me. The fear, despair, loss of life, the overwhelming feelings without support took over. I had no idea how to process my emotions or feelings. I've previously mentioned that I was not fluent in feelings. I did not grow up talking about feelings or acknowledging them. In this situation, I hit a wall of overwhelm and could not stop crying. I had to get out of there. I returned to the office, packed up for the day, and headed home. On leaving the office, I could not form a sentence to express that I was leaving for the day. I had fallen entirely into a trauma response without knowing what a trauma response was. I could not speak and was overtaken with tears; my body ached.

What was going on with me? I could not explain it to myself. Once I got home, I became more emotionally regulated. I needed to take time and reflect on what was going on with me: Why was I responding the way I was to the situation? Being curious about the origins of the situations assists us with getting in touch with the foundations of where these responses are rooted.

In this situation, I carried historical, cultural, collective, and secondary trauma into this situation about a Black man who was bullied and treated badly. It was like I was personally suffering. I could not separate what had happened to him and what I was feeling myself. The anger and blaming of the institution represented unsafety and unfairness. How did this project so deeply inside me? I was puzzled.

The first thing that happened is I felt in my body that something was not right. I felt it when I was asked to go to the location and after I got there. Instead of taking time for myself, I rushed in to assist. When I was met with anger, uncontrollable tears, and panic from the management, I continued to push forward to assist. It was when I was on the verge of tears and uncontrollable sadness that I decided to remove myself. I ignored my body and therefore pushed myself deep into a trauma response. I hope this story illustrates how vital the connection with your body is; it is the first step toward healing.

I Am Not Enough

In my upbringing, a lot of attention was given to how everyone looked, the outside job. My grandparents were farmers and lived in poverty, although no one ever, ever said so. The narrative is that everything was provided, clothes were made, the family worked together to earn money, and all was well. In my healing, I needed to discover what was behind some of the body image and clothes issues I incorporated into my life. Clothing was a big deal growing up. Fancy dresses by designers were the norm. If you can imagine a hippylike person, me, in a family that loved designer clothing and fancy shoes. I have flat feet, so I love comfy shoes, and for clothes, comfort is a priority. I wore the outfits that were approved and was shamed or bullied for any outfit that was not approved of by my family. This foundational clothing ideal played out in many ways as I reached adulthood. I wore clothes I did not necessarily love and dressed to meet the needs of those around me. The next scenario, however, will describe how I eventually learned to take care of myself and not fall back into the trauma.

I traveled to see a family member receive an award. Of course, I bought an outfit that was appropriate for the occasion. One of my family members saw my outfit and had a very strong opinion about my shoes. The shoes I had picked were not good enough to be worn to the event. This resulted in a family discussion about my shoes and a strong urging that I wear something else. This was very upsetting to me. In the past, I would not have felt the rejection and judgment about my wardrobe, I would have done what the group wanted. Now, I was able to pause, take a breath, and ask myself what was best for me, and what was at the foundation of this control over how I dress. How would I even make the connection between generational poverty in my family to the shoes I am wearing today? I was horrified; I was a grown adult, and I was being harassed about the shoes I had chosen because of unknown factors of trauma from the past. This fact gave me the ability to feel compassion for my family and for myself.

I made a boundary about my shoes. I was wearing them and I did not want to hear anything else about it. It was important that I understood the trauma response and my relationship to it. My focus was not on changing my family members or correcting their behavior. I learned to take care of myself in relationship to them. I did not overexplain, curry favor, or hold resentment for the mistreatment. I went to the event and wore my outfit as planned. I was comfortable with my body, mind, and spirit. Trauma healing is about compassion for yourself and others. It is not necessary to overly focus on others; it is important to know how to take care of ourselves.

Once you are connected to your body and once you notice when your body is communicating, you can identify results of trauma experiences. By noting the different kinds of trauma, it will assist you in identifying what is going on inside of you. Being able to identify feelings in the body is the first step to tuning in to a situation where something could feel off. It has been a journey of discovery to realize I am worth the time I spend healing trauma responses. These situations do not just occur in family systems; they occur in employment, community groups, and in relationships. The subtleties of the feelings are there. I had always ignored them though. These ideals of self-criticism came from somewhere. I was not born with them. These messages lived inside of me, and I thought they were my thoughts, and they weren't. Trauma has a way of lingering and morphing into other problems.

I had high blood pressure as a result of a stressful work environment. It took me a while to realize this invisible change because I had lived with my coping mechanisms for so long. On the outside, I thought my coping strategies were working, but I actually experienced physical issues from mental and emotional stress.

In the next section, you will reflect and discover areas where you may need healing. In the first writing prompt, you will write about experiences that continue to live in your body and mind. You will also be prompted to use the list to help you think about themes of possible healing. After using the list for identification, you will write about what stood out before moving on to the end of the chapter review.

Journal Reflection: Behaviors and Feelings

Use the prompts below to capture your reflections about the previous sections in your journal. These guiding questions are provided to assist you in this reflection process.

- Write about an experience you have had that has not quite gone away.
- Examine the following list to identify things that crop up in your life. Try not to think about your answers, let your body choose. What do you identify with?
    - Working too much
    - Bouts of sadness

- Negative self-talk
- Feeling down
- Hard to express emotions
- Feel like life is happening to you
- Powerlessness
- Physical problems
- Easily irritated
- Mood swings
- Comfort food
- Exercise for relaxation
- Drinking to relax
- Racing thoughts
- Quick to anger
- Experience high highs
- Experience low lows
- Dishonesty
- Thoughts of revenge
- Inability to focus
- Inability to stop moving
- Blanking out/daydreaming
- Fantasizing
- Critical of others/self
- Addiction
- Numbness
- Minimizing things

- Making a big deal out of small things

- Hypervigilance; on guard

- Victimhood/martyrdom

- Lack of empathy

- Physical aggression

- Learned helplessness

- Abuse in family system

• What stood out about the checklist activity?

• What are some actions or feelings you do not understand about yourself?

Self-Care Tools: Body Regulation and Calming

The purpose of self-care tools is to help you regulate and calm your body for overall health. These suggestions include tools I have found helpful in my growth and development. These tools do not replace a doctor's care and medical attention. The tools are provided as a supplement to your Wellness Tool Kit if the tool fits. Check with your doctor or healthcare provider if you have questions about whether a particular self-care tool is appropriate.

Finger Holds

Finger holding is a helpful tool to use to reset your body from stress. Using information about traditional Chinese medicine regarding meridians, which are acupuncture points and a system that aligns to balance energy in the body, finger holds help reset emotions and feelings. I have used finger holds in meetings, holding my hands under the table and in public places to assist me resetting when emotions arise. Each finger on your hand represents a group of emotions.

To use the finger hold method, pick a hand that you will apply pressure to; you will use the other hand to apply firm pressure to each finger. You can see each finger's emotional connection on the following graphic. A common practice is to sit quietly and snugly wrap your hand around your thumb to start.

After acquiring a firm grip, slowly breathe in and out, focusing on what you would like instead of the feelings you are experiencing. Breathe in and out slowly for a few minutes, focusing your thoughts on calmness. The thumb represents grief, tears, and emotional pain. Imagine yourself not having those emotions; imagine peace and inner calm instead.

Move to the next finger when you are ready and repeat the same steps. Wrap your fingers firmly around your index finger and breathe in and out, focusing on replacing fear and panic with calm and tranquility. The words you choose are up to you. Modify this tool however it fits you best. To breathe through this refocusing tool, you could even take ten minutes on a break at work.

I have used this in meetings when harmful information was being shared. If my body began to feel panic, I would squeeze all my fingers together under the table and take deep breaths. This is one of my favorite go-to tools.

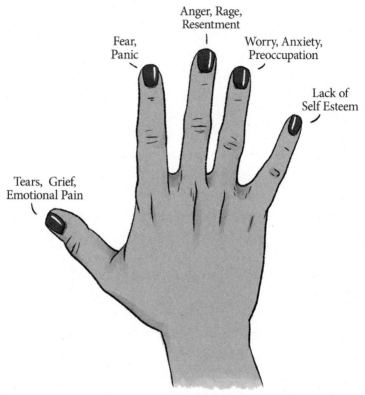

Anger, Rage,
Resentment

Fear,
Panic

Worry, Anxiety,
Preoccupation

Lack of
Self Esteem

Tears, Grief,
Emotional Pain

Finger Holds

Emotional Tapping

I first learned emotional tapping from Carolyn Yoder at the Center for Justice and Peacebuilding. Dr. Yoder asked if anyone in the class had an emotional discomfort, pain, or ache they wanted to focus on in the tapping exercise. At the time, I did not believe what she was going to lead us in would work, and I was not brave enough to share in front of the group that I had horrible lower back pain. A class member shared their discomfort, and Dr. Yoder began to lead us through a tapping sequence on our hand, head, face, collarbone, chest, and side of our body. After several rounds of tapping, we stopped, and my back pain was gone. I could not believe it. How could this tapping take away something that has been bothering me since before the beginning of the course? I was a believer and added emotional tapping to my tools to reset my body whether I knew what was bothering me or not. The funny thing about that back pain is that it did not return until it was time to go home.

To begin emotional tapping, sit in an isolated quiet space and breathe in and out deeply. There are many sequences of emotional tapping; this one begins at the side of your hand.

Steps to Emotional Tapping

These steps have been adapted with permission from the EFT materials of Gary Flint, PhD. Emotional tapping is a resource to use when you are distressed or experiencing anxiety, worry, bad memories, or negative self-talk. If your body is expressing discomfort from your emotional responses, this is a good tool to try.

1. Side of hand: Using your index and middle fingers, tap seven to nine times.

2. Above beginning of eyebrow: Using your index and middle fingers, tap seven to nine times.

3. End of eyebrow: Using your index and middle fingers, tap seven to nine times.

4. Below eye: Using your index and middle fingers, tap seven to nine times.

5. Under nose: Using your index and middle fingers, tap seven to nine times.

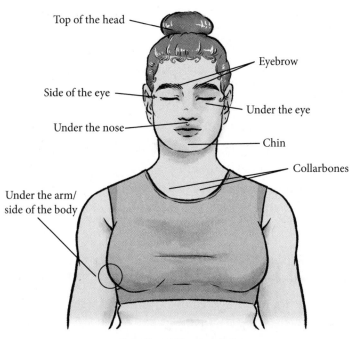

Emotional Tapping Points

6. Under lips: Using your index and middle fingers, tap seven to nine times.

7. Under arm: Using your index and middle fingers, tap seven to nine times.

8. Below collarbone: Using your index and middle fingers, tap seven to nine times.

Once you have gone through the sequence, go back to the side of your hand and state:

Even though I am feeling problems in my body, I am okay and accept myself.

Repeat the sequence until you feel calmer and more at peace.

Once you do come to the end of your tapping sequence, put light pressure on the area right above your heart and give yourself a final positive affirmation.

Affirmations

Here are some affirmations you can try, or create ones that feel positive and supportive for you.

I am courageous, I love myself and my healing journey.
I have hope for my healing and well-being.
I am filled with love in and out of me.
Peace is my comforter.
I thrive to live in peace, wrapped in loving-kindness.

Meditation

Meditation is when your mind and body slow down. The science behind meditation shows that as you are meditating, your brain waves move to different frequencies, which are measured in Hertz (Hz). Brain waves start at Gamma when you are operating at optimal performance and can be as low as Delta when your brain is resting and not working. See the following chart for details.

BRAINWAVE STATES

Brainwave States	Speed and Purpose
Delta (less than 0.5–3 Hz)	Delta state is the slowest brain wave.
Theta (3–8 Hz)	Theta state brain waves are slow and increase when you are awake and focusing.
Alpha (8–13 Hz)	Alpha state is when your brain is relaxed but alert yet not processing information.
Beta (13–40 Hz)	Beta state is when the brain is alert and is working processing external information.
Gamma (40–100 Hz)	Gamma state is when the brain is concentrating and reaches its peak concentration.

Your goal for meditation is to bring your awareness and meditation to Alpha or Theta brain waves.

Binaural Beats

Binaural beats are the use of auditory frequencies at two different levels. The frequencies are used to assist the brain waves in moving into relaxation. Try the use of binaural beats to enhance your meditation practice. Whether it is with the sound of the waves, waterfalls, wind in the trees, or other nature sounds, use this opportunity to take your meditative practice to the next level of supporting your healing journey.

Rituals

Let's revisit and add to the rituals introduced in the previous chapter.

Morning

When you open your eyes from slumber, take a deep breath in and slowly blow it out. By this time, you may have already established a gratitude practice. In addition to the gratitude practice, take time to ground yourself before you start your day. Try rubbing your feet on the floor and using your intent to push energy into the floor down into the earth and then pull new energy from the earth through the floor up into your body. Feel the new energy move up through your feet, up your body, and through your crown. Take a deep breath and begin your day.

Noon

Around noon, stop and take quiet time for yourself. Prioritize yourself and take time to meditate. Take time to follow a guided meditation or practice deep intentional breathing.

Evening

In the evening, before dinner or at bedtime, take a moment to breathe in positive thoughts. Recite a prayer, an inspirational quote, or a meditative guide.

Chapter Summary

This chapter discussed the sources of trauma that can live in our energy centers. There are so many sources and intersections of trauma that one could get overwhelmed learning about them all. Practical examples were given of how a trauma response can show up in day-to-day interactions. Lastly, self-care tools were given to assist in calming the body. The overall goal in healing trauma is to pause before a trauma response to care for yourself. Tuning in to your body and knowing the sources of trauma is the foundation for noticing our thinking.

CHAPTER FOUR
MIND PATTERNS OF TRAUMA

The previous chapters reviewed the foundational information and steps you'll need to fully participate in the healing work to come. The result of this work will be a direct reflection of what you put into it. I took one step at a time and this book is set up in the way I walked toward healing. In the introduction, I discussed why and how the truth about trauma was revealed in my life. While chapter 1 reviewed information about trauma as a science with real-life experiences and examples, chapter 3 discussed the kinds of trauma sources and how each can be hidden in our everyday lives. In this chapter, we will review ways to interrupt trauma and move toward wellness and self-care.

To explore the places in our lives that have been affected by harmful experiences, we started at Level 1 of the Three Levels of Healing, as shown in graphic 3 on page 48.

Level 1 is where we get in touch with our bodies. Chapter 2 recommended suggestions on ways to do so. By now, a clear connection of listening to your body should be established. If you find yourself not sure whether you are connected to your body, review chapters 1 through 3. Use the information below as indications of body connection:

- Noticing that your gut is not comfortable with people, places, or things
- Noticing body aches and pains that come and go when you change locations
- Loss of appetite
- Increase of appetite
- Headaches
- Stomachaches
- Fidgeting
- Hypervigilance

The most important thing is to notice these nuances in your body and not ignore them. By this point in the book, you are hopefully spending quality time with yourself quietly. This special time will assist you in providing your body and mind with rest and rejuvenation.

The next step for us is to understand and train our minds; we are moving on to Level 2 in the three levels of healing. This is a very important step for healing. The examination of mind patterns in Level 2 is vital to healing and self-actualization. Do you realize all the thoughts that go through your mind?

The time to sit quietly is a precious gift, and the next step to learning the truth about trauma is to understand your situation and utilize the three levels to interrupt trauma responses.

Using the level system helps you go back to the healing aspects of interrupting trauma in your body. To review, Level 1 helps us understand how our body responds to trauma and identifies those responses and tools for healing the body, mind, and spirit. After acknowledging and connecting with our body, we move into Level 2 to interrupt subconscious belief patterns in our thinking. Acknowledgment of trauma in the body makes space to witness our belief system. In Level 2, we will examine beliefs through our everyday experiences. Our belief system is closely associated with our body functions. What we believe can be based on conscious or subconscious beliefs. We will become curious about our feelings and daily interactions. We can uncover past harms and discover strengths. The experiences we remember or do not remember can be identified and resolved through simple-to-use reflection tools in Level 2.

Lastly, to hold on to our learning and reflections, Level 3 will help us continue to break free and pave new roads in our body, mind, and spirit. By creating new healing pathways, the body and mind make space for the spirit. Paving a new road is breaking free from trauma, and it works best when there is a community of support. In Level 3, we will identify what kind of support fits you best for physical, emotional, and spiritual support. This step integrates body, mind, and spirit tools to build the Breaking Free Cycle. This cycle includes the useful tools discovered at each level and combines them into a pathway one can follow and review when changes need to occur. This level provides assistance, suggestions for support, and guidelines to sustain new ways of living as you experience more positive energy.

Noticing Your Thoughts

Your thoughts are so powerful, even though you may know it does not stop you from negative self-talk and deep-rooted belief systems. The best of us has deeply hidden beliefs in our psyche and energy systems. I first addressed this thought system when I examined my belief systems. My biggest challenge was accepting that I may have belief systems contradicting my wishes and dreams. Today, I live with a quiet head and calm stomach. I do not have the negative thoughts plaguing me because I removed them. They no longer run the show in my head. It is a feeling of freedom, and it is available to all.

The first step in noticing your thoughts is to pay attention to them. The silent and personal thoughts are the ones we will be focusing on. During your day, pay attention to any thoughts that are unloving, unkind, or not thoughtful. Look for mean, unkind, judgmental, sarcastic, bullying, and down-putting thoughts. You want to separate these thoughts from who you are because these thoughts are not you. Think about the nagging voice that is the critic. It is not yours. Whose is it? If the voice is not saying you are great, successful, and amazing, it is not your voice. Do you wonder why these thoughts are not positive? My thoughts never tell me that I will win the lotto and all my dreams will come true! Things like affirmations and energy work are the tools to remove what is not serving your body, mind, and spirit. It is well worth the work.

We have set a foundation in your body awareness to take the next step of noticing what is going on in your thinking.

Journal Reflection: Critical Voices

Use the prompt below to capture your reflections about the previous section in your journal. This prompt is provided to assist you in this reflection process.

Take a minute and reflect on whose voice is nagging you not to be late or criticizing anything about you or how you live your life.

These voices have marked your systems with harm, and invariably they somehow became part of your thinking. What we want to do in this chapter is extract the unkind voices that have taken a place in our energy systems and examine them.

Personal Experience: Interrupting a Critical Voice

Interrupting the critical and unkind voices in your inner world is a massive step toward healing. Here's a story of how interrupting a harmful voice led me to feel safe and loved in my body.

One of the first voices that I interrupted was the one that criticized my weight. When I was younger, my weight was a topic of discussion in my family. Everyone's weight was a topic of discussion—all the women. As a child, I would hear comments about my weight regularly. As an adult, I still heard comments about my weight on a regular basis from my family members. At one family gathering when I was college age, a male relative called me over to him to share something. As I got closer, he gestured to lean in so he could whisper something in my ear; he said, "Lose some weight." I was horrified; he had just called me across the room to tell me to lose weight.

The voice that continued to put me down about my looks had been implanted in me for many years. I found I was unkind to myself about all my outside appearance: hair, clothes, weight, style, and so on. This profound harm required me to recognize the thoughts and ask myself, whose voice is this? Whose voice is this? This action required vigilance to replace the voice and belief system that accompanied it. The belief was that I was unacceptable, that I did not belong, was unloved, and unwanted.

I replaced that belief with the belief that I am secure and loved, and I practiced things that I loved and surrounded myself with people who loved me through their actions. I interrupted the thoughts as they came into my mind and slowly diminished them. It has been a long time since I have had a cycle of those thoughts. By staying connected to my body, I refine my belief systems to live in peace.

If you have ever experienced shock and rudeness, the pain of the interaction lingers. Trauma experiences are the same way. It does not have to be life threatening to stay with you and follow you through your life. The simple truth is all it had to do was hurt. Many of us have had experiences that hurt us through the years. The sad thing is many of us seem to think that harmful energy just goes away. It does not go away. It is much like throwing trash in the back seat of the car—eventually it will come into the front seat. The work in front of us is to take out the trash. In our case, the trash is the harm. We want to take it out, so we do not continue to harm ourselves directly or indirectly, and we do not want to bring harm to others directly or indirectly. When we heal harm, we are more able to see others and be ourselves with love. How glorious would it be if in community we worked to better the society for us all? I think that would be amazing.

Now we are going to roll up our sleeves and be willing to settle ourselves from our busy lives and become curious about our needs and healing.

A good place to start is by examining how many unkind thoughts you have a day about yourself, someone else, an institution, a television show, an action, gestures, and so on. Anything that is not positive. Realistically this may seem out of the box. Think about this for a minute. How will we get the real suffering out of our heart if we ignore the day-to-day experiences? Be courageous and count your negative thoughts from the time you get up until lunch. These are thoughts you would not want repeated. These are thoughts that you do not have to say out loud. If you are wondering how to identify negative thoughts, ask yourself if you would say that thought to your most loved friend. And determine whether the thought is judging yourself or others. A good marker for a thought that is negative is by answering the following questions with a yes or no answer:

- Is it thoughtful?
- Is it kind?
- Is it necessary?

Take note of how your thoughts engage you. This action is the first step in noticing past experiences in your everyday life.

Journal Reflection: Thoughts and Belief System

Use the prompts below to capture your reflections about the previous section in your journal. These guiding questions are provided to assist you in this reflection process.

- Take a moment to reflect on your thoughts and belief system. In your journal, write the first thing that comes to mind. What do you think about most?

- Have you ever observed your thoughts? Take a morning to observe your thoughts. Write your reflections in your journal.

- Is your deepest belief about you and your life positive and joyful? If yes, describe your thoughts. If not, describe those thoughts.

- What are you most positive about?

- What are you most negative about?

- Have others in life not believed in you?

- Do you think about those people?

- What do you know about your body alerts in situations that are not comfortable?

Examining Your Mind Patterns

An excellent place to start to examine your thoughts is by examining how many times you judge yourself. It could look like this:

That was dumb! Come on, stupid! Leave it to me to screw this up! You know, at my age...I am so old. I am not good at _____. I am so fat. It was probably my fault. I am sure I messed this up somehow. That was a mistake, dumbass. What the hell was I thinking? I knew I would mess this up.

Or it could look like this:

What the hell are they doing? That person makes me crazy. I cannot stand their voice. This place is the worst. I cannot believe how stupid these people are! Look at what they are wearing! Who let them out of the house? Now that is downright ugly. They look like a dog. How can they live there?

Or it could look like this behavior:

- Correcting people in your head while they are talking
- Finishing sentences, having another conversation, over-powering others while they are talking
- Cycling in thinking of a situation or conversation that has already happened
- Reliving situations over and over again
- Daydreaming and checking out in conversations, during downtime, meetings, for enjoyment, etc.
- Fantasizing about a situation, person, place, or thing, positive or negative
- Thinking angry, revenge, martyr thoughts
- Every positive task or action is met with a defeatist comment

The information about your thoughts is not exhaustive. There are many ways your mind seems to go off on its own without your permission. What we want to do is control our mind, remove unpleasant thoughts, and replace them with peace.

The first set of comments on the previous page represents the internal dialogue of self-hatred. In chapter 2, I discussed the negative voices from childhood that sink in and become part of adulthood. These self-defeating comments are what happens to those childhood narratives. Instead of adults saying them to us, we harm ourselves with harsh thoughts. Remember the STAR cycles of violence (graphic 2) from chapter 2? Look at the following graphic. Our internal thoughts are on a cycle.

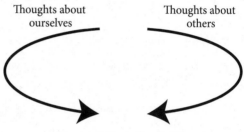

Thoughts about ourselves

Thoughts about others

Internal Thoughts Cycle

Negative thoughts do not produce positive thoughts. Negative, unkind, unthoughtful thoughts produce the same for you and others. Like the cycles of trauma that were discussed in chapter 2, these thoughts produce a cycle of unhappiness. If we are not throwing zingers at ourselves, it is more likely that the rude comments and thoughts are being projected outside of ourselves onto others. This action is the cycle of harm that is a product of living with trauma. Take a minute here and take a breath. Watch your thinking at this moment. If your thoughts begin to jump into wondering how you could be this way, *stop it*. The change occurs by stopping those thoughts when they happen or right away telling yourself that it's not true or that you take it back. Receiving information about negative thoughts can produce more negative thoughts! The information you have received is the opening of a door to free your body, mind, and spirit.

How to Interrupt Thoughts

In order to interrupt these thoughts, it is important to watch for them and become in relationship with the thoughts. Each negative thought is like a slap in the face to yourself whether it is about you or someone else. Yes, comments about someone else are a slap in the face to you. This is one of the biggest reasons I began to examine my thoughts. I wanted to be kinder to myself; therefore, I needed to be kinder to others. I thought negative, judgmental, and mean things about other people. They did not hear me. I thought as long as you do not say anything out loud, then it is fine. I found that not to be true. When I was judging, ridiculing, and thinking unkind thoughts, it was hurting me. It was my unhealed trauma that produced a negative shadow and projection.

The truth about trauma is that it is hidden but not silent. My actions, thoughts, and how I saw others were affected by the traumatic experiences in my life. I wanted to be free, kind, and not on edge in life so I focused on my thoughts and began to interrupt them with the tools I am sharing. Yet, for some reason, it is difficult to stop saying or thinking negatively. A couple of actions helped me with the struggle. One, I continued to stay in touch with my body. I was meditating, getting movement regularly, and being creative or doing what I loved. Second, I removed myself from any friend or acquaintance who was negative. Would I want anyone to speak to my good friend the way I was speaking to myself?

To interrupt negative thoughts:

- Stay connected to your body (meditation, exercise, good diet, hydration)
- Pause when the thoughts arise
- Say to yourself, *That is not true, Stop it,* or, *I take that back*
- Write the thought down, cross out your thought, and write a positive thought to replace it:
  - ~~You are so dumb~~
  - You are intelligent and bright

In the next sections, we will learn how to notice negative thought patterns more closely.

My work with many different modalities taught me different parts of my healing story. In my studies as a life coach, we often discussed the shadow of the subconscious. I learned to look at my everyday life and notice the hidden shadow beliefs. I was always encouraged to be curious about what was happening instead of freaking out or coming to my own conclusions. Being curious takes courage because you are saying, "Universe, I don't have an answer, but I trust one will be coming to me." Use your curiosity and trust in this section as you learn to look deeper into past harms. Also be curious about the joy and happiness you experience. Capitalize on the positives in your life too.

Now let's introduce a powerful healing tool called the Thinking Map. This tool has helped me realize, reflect, and rewrite to remove parts of my experiences that no longer work for my lifestyle. It has assisted me in interrupting negative belief patterns and rewriting new positive beliefs. Below are the steps to follow to walk yourself through the Thinking Map (adapted from concepts in Conscious Freedom Life Coaching, 2008).

Using the Thinking Map

Say a positive intention and affirmation prayer before you begin:

Allow me to see the truth and be a better soul.

Step 1: Pick a situation that has bothered you. The one criterion for the subject is something that rubbed you the wrong way.

Step 2: Write what happened in the situation. Write the bottom line of the situation. This can be difficult to write because most of us have the story or narrative wrapped around the core of the situation. You will get better at this step with practice.

Step 3: Write how you felt about the situation. This can be tricky too because sometimes it is difficult to simply describe the feelings. List the feelings in this step.

Step 4: Write what your deep belief about yourself is. This step can be puzzling until you get used to it. Based on the situation and your feelings, what is the deeper belief about yourself? After you have had time to reflect, pick one of the descriptions:

HELPLESS

UNACCEPTABLE

DISADVANTAGED

Or

_____ *(you fill in a word)*

This last question is a difficult one because it is hard to think that you may have a belief system that is not supporting who you are. Take a deep breath, close your eyes, and the answer will come to you.

Step 5: Was there anything that happened in your early years or in your life that would cause you to believe you are what you have chosen?

List your answers. Look at what you have written. Ask yourself if these feelings could come from other challenging experiences. Does this situation remind you of unresolved feelings from the past? Your feelings are more likely historical. It is in your past and not what your life is like today. This step removes the subconscious belief from hiding and puts it front and center. In this step, you are shining a light on something untrue.

Step 6: Rewrite the narrative. In this step, you communicate that this belief is not true and you write all that is true about you. Write the evidence from your life that your hidden belief is false. Cross out this belief (literally) and write a new replacement belief about yourself.

Thinking Map Example

Remember my story about going to a meeting when I did not know why it was being called or what my role in the meeting would need to be? I was uncomfortable attending the meeting without any prior knowledge about it. In the story, I used the Thinking Map to resolve the situation. Below is an illustration of how the Thinking Map works.

Using the Thinking Map, let's break this example down step by step:

Step 1: Pick a situation that has bothered you.

Work-related issue.

Step 2: Write what happened in the situation. Write the bottom line of the situation.

> *I was scheduled for a meeting without any additional information about it.*

Step 3: Write how you felt about the situation.

> *Moody, mad, frustrated, angry, nervous, worried, cautious, empty.*

Step 4: Ask the question: What is the deeper belief about yourself?

HELPLESS: I felt like I did not have any choices in this meeting. The meeting was happening to me.

Step 5: Was there anything that happened in your early years or in your life that would cause you to believe you are *HELPLESS*?

I was adopted at four years old by my mom's husband.

I did not know my biological dad growing up.

My mom was a single mom.

I moved a lot as a kid: new school, places to live.

Is it possible that the feeling I was having is not what is going on today but feeling from struggles in the past? Yes. It is possible that these early feelings are coming up in this adult situation. Yes, the unsettled feeling of not knowing what was going to happen. Maybe that feeling is one I had as a very young person, an unknown feeling.

Step 6: Rewrite the narrative.

I do not know the origins or the purpose of this meeting. It is okay not to know what is going to happen. I will be safe and secure. I have all the skills and tools to take care of myself. If I need help, I have people I can reach out to.

~~I am helpless because I do not know what is happening.~~

I am capable, safe, and able to take care of myself in this setting and all settings. If I require help, I have support I can contact.

The amazing thing about this tool is that I could feel immediate relief in my body once I found the source of my discomfort. This tool assisted me in this situation and other situations with similar feelings. I experienced new energy from this newfound awareness.

Using this Thinking Map has brought me a lot of freedom from past harmful feelings and experiences hidden in my life.

Deep Belief Systems

Where do deep beliefs come from, and how do you explore getting to know them? The programming or beliefs come from our experiences. Programming refers to patterns that become part of your life practices. Deep belief systems can also come from positive or negative experiences from today or generations in the past. This area is one that requires attention because the beliefs are so ingrained in your body that it seems like they are part of you. It takes some time to realize a deep belief may be the culprit of a challenging situation. According to Boni Lonnsburry's *The Map: To Our Responsive Universe—Where Dreams Really Do Come True*, beliefs fall into three categories: surface, ingrained, and core beliefs. A belief that is on the surface is not deep or doesn't have a long history. A surface belief could be something like "cooking is hard for me" or "it's too difficult to backpack." Surface beliefs are easier to change. To change these beliefs, you simply change how you think about them. Instead of thinking that cooking is hard, you begin to tell yourself that cooking is easy or simple. You reprogram your thoughts by repeating to yourself daily the opposite of that thought; in this example, that would be "cooking is easy." You may follow up to affirm that new thought by taking a basic cooking class with a friend. Surface beliefs are simple. Like most transformative work, it is best to write down your thoughts and what you would like to change. Changing surface beliefs can be transformative. You have the power to create what you like. One positive step is an examination of surface beliefs that do not fit the ideals you have about your life.

The second kind of belief is an ingrained belief. An ingrained belief is one that has a foothold in our lives and lives in our subconscious mind. It could be programming that occurred growing up. It could come from generations of family beliefs, teachers, religious leaders, or authority figures. Think about all the places where you may receive information that is seemingly true. When I think of this, there are many ways social media, television, films, and societal norms can communicate the foundation of ingrained beliefs. An ingrained belief can be "I will not get promoted," "I will not find a mate," "There are not safe places to live," or "I am not good enough to move up in my job."

The thing about ingrained beliefs is that they are coupled by a grain of fear and false information. Somewhere in your life, information was given to you that became a foundation for your belief. For example, I had one of these beliefs about trusting people outside of my family. How did that thought become an ingrained belief? For me, the idea of not trusting people outside of my family centered on several ingrained beliefs. One was that people outside of my family are not trustworthy. That is not true. Many people are good people. Another belief I had was that if I was to succeed in life, everything was up to me. That was not true either. The universe is massive and my intentions and goals work in tandem with a universal force. I am part of it, but I am not the center of the universe nor control all things.

You can imagine how stressful these ingrained beliefs made day-to-day living. With those ingrained beliefs, it was easy for me not to believe in myself or humanity. I am sure that my family system did not project these beliefs to cause harm. When examining the context and the time of origination, I can imagine that those beliefs probably kept my family safe during a time when safety was paramount. Ingrained beliefs can be changed. To transform ingrained beliefs, it requires you to utilize the tools you have been using in this book.

Journal to collect and examine your ingrained beliefs during your healing journey. Journal about each one and its origination. Ask yourself: Where did this belief come from? Write down the ingrained beliefs and replacement beliefs. Complete a calming meditation that takes you to your safe place. This place is somewhere you love and feel at home, safe, and cared for. Visualize all the things that bring you joy in this place (flowers, animals, guides, angels, etc.), your special healing place. For me, it is a beautiful waterfall and calm beach. Begin your removal of ingrained beliefs by saying the White Light Prayer. Ask the universe for guidance and healing before you visualize each ingrained belief, taking time to sit with each before you say, "I release this belief, it is deleted." Draw a line through the ingrained belief on your paper or journal and write the new belief. Read the new belief out loud. Repeat this process for each ingrained belief until you have finished going through your list. Keep your new list of beliefs handy on an index card or in a notes app on your phone and review it as much as you can the first few weeks.

The third type of belief is core beliefs, which is very deep and affects every part of you. These kinds of thoughts perpetuate beliefs of unworthiness, deprivation, unlovable, and helplessness. Core beliefs live in the conscious and unconscious mind. These are the kind of beliefs that produce negative thoughts, actions, words, and ideas about yourself.

In my coaching practice, I often ask a client: Whose voice is saying those things to you? Oftentimes my question is followed by a pause and a name does emerge. Core beliefs are the hardest to remove because they live in the root shadow, which is the foundational beginning. The root stands for the root chakras. Chakras or energy centers will be reviewed in chapter 5. The root chakra is the first energy center; it is the energy center in our body that says you belong, are safe and loved. When a belief is centered in belonging, it is a very deep belief that is not even conscious. Events that occur in early life or even during conception can translate into core beliefs. The challenge of core beliefs is that the thought seems like it originates within you. In a way, it does originate from within, but it is not true information. The quiet time of meditation assists in interrupting these beliefs and making room for the truth and light to be seen and heard. The best way to approach core beliefs is to examine base ideas about your life that you believe to be unequivocally true. These ideas do not serve your well-being in any way.

Examples of core beliefs are as follows:

- "I never get what I want."
- "I am useless at work."
- "I am unlovable."
- "No one wants to be with me."
- "I could disappear, and no one would notice."
- "I don't matter in (fill in the blank)."

To begin reflecting on core beliefs, examine places in your life where you want to see change: relationships, work, negative self-talk, or harsh statements that you believe about yourself. As you continue to travel on your healing journey, layers of trauma will fall away and new areas for healing will appear. Core beliefs may be found within those deeper layers. When they do appear, you can heal them too.

To get rid of core beliefs, it can be helpful to spend some time to see where the message entered your system. It could come from past generations or lifetimes ago. When you are curious, the energy of information can come to you. It is not necessary to force healing. It comes at its own rate. Spend some time exploring where your core belief originated and try to understand how it got lodged in your system. I have found this very helpful in moving the old belief out and understanding how it emerged in the first place. You may not find it, but you should still try. The belief must be replaced with what you want in your life instead.

For core beliefs, use the same process as you did with the ingrained belief. Journal about the beliefs and what you want to replace them with in your life. Again, find a quiet place and start with the White Light Prayer. Visualize and take yourself to your sacred place surrounded by all you love. With the core belief, you will need a special guide, angel, ancestor, or protector to accompany you. Your guide will take you into a dark forest and you will follow them through the forest until you get to a clearing. In the clearing, visualize a broken-down shack. Follow your guide into the old building and find the room in which your belief began. Even if you do not remember, follow and go into the room. If you remember, you will see the people who originated the belief, and you may see how the core belief started.

Watch whatever happens in that room. Remember your guide is with you and you are not alone. A bag will appear in your hand; this is the core belief and all the feelings that come with it. Say to those in the room, whether you can see them or not, "I have something that belongs to you." Hand back the core belief to the people who gave it to you. Back out of the room and follow your guide out of the shack back through the dark forest and to your special place. You will feel different, lighter, and with more positive energy. Sit in your special place with all you love until you are ready to come out of the meditation. Your new belief was written before you went into meditation. In your journal, cross out the old belief and read the new belief out loud. Post it close by and read it regularly for several weeks. Every day, breathe in the new belief and new energy.

Belief systems are complicated and are wired into our body, mind, and spirit. When you begin to work on healing, all the information you need to know will come to you. It does not come all at once. It comes slowly and it comes to you when you need it. Think about belief systems as outdated clothes. You are upgrading your body, mind, and spirit; you are going shopping to upgrade your wardrobe accordingly. It may be difficult to accept that you believed things about yourself that were not positive. Over time, if you were told you were horrible at math, you may have internalized that belief. If you listen closely today, you can hear adults say they are bad at math. Why would someone be saying that as an adult? Somewhere in their experiences, a programmed thought taught them that math was not their strength. Remember implicit and explicit memories? Wherever the idea comes from, it becomes lodged in beliefs. Uncovering unwanted beliefs means continuing to be curious about ideas, ways of knowing, and actions you would like to change in your life. Use the journal prompts in this book to examine places that you would like to be different. Through the examination of belief systems, you will remove and discard unhelpful beliefs.

Journal Reflection: Deep Beliefs

Use the prompts below to capture your reflections about the previous section in your journal. These guiding prompts are provided to assist you in this reflection process.

- List the situations you find bothersome in your life.
- List the things you are proud about in your life.
- I am curious about changing the way I _____.
- I believe I know all I need to know about myself except

  _____.

- I am open to learning more about myself because

  _____.

- The reasons I love myself are_____

  _____.

Self-Care Tools: Deepening Your Practice

The following self-care tools are foundational to healing. The self-care tools in this section were suggestions made earlier in the book, and here, each is discussed in more detail as you continue to build on and deepen your practice. The intention is to provide more information to encourage you to hone your practice in each area to support your healing journey. Knowing the information is the first part of supporting yourself. You need to engage with each topic and begin to practice some form of self-care in each area. The energy around supporting self-care is a loving effort. Take time to devise a plan or thoughts on each self-care tool. It is okay if you do not know what direction to move in. The important part is to reflect and consider how you will care for yourself in these areas moving forward.

In the following sections, I also share my journey with each topic and how I was able to use each to care more deeply for myself. I'll also share additional suggestions and reflections to assist you in building foundations for your healing journey.

Sleep

Sleep is vital to the care of your body and brain function. It is easy to dismiss the attention rest needs. When your body sleeps, it restores your muscles and boosts your immune system. Part of caring for your body is to provide yourself with quality sleep. Sleep is one of the first areas I focused on in healing the body, mind, and spirit. I used to ignore sleep patterns. I did not understand the importance of the rest my body needed.

I began to focus on the number of hours I slept each night. Knowing the number of hours that worked best for my body was essential to my day-to-day life. I began to make decisions for my schedule and nighttime rituals based on what worked well for my body.

The next area I looked at was the quality of my sleep, how long I slept, and whether I woke up rested. I learned that my body sleeps better when I monitor my sleep habits and sleep quality. Today, it is easy to use electronics such as mobile devices, sleep apps, exercise monitors, or personal sleep logs to help improve your sleep. I use an app to monitor the quality of my sleep.

- Focus on keeping a regular schedule.
- Monitor what you eat or drink before bedtime. Avoid:
  - Large meals
  - Alcohol
  - Caffeine
- Create a sleeping environment that is restful, peaceful, and flows with your personal comfort.
- Minimize electronics before bedtime.

- Exercise regularly.
- Avoid heavy workouts in the evening.

Answer the following prompts on your current sleep habits and patterns.

- How do you prioritize sleep?
- Do you have a regular schedule?
- Do you have a typical bedtime or any night rituals?
- Describe your plan to enhance your sleep routines.

Exercise

Exercise is essential to maintaining a good connection with your body, mind, and spirit. It is necessary because your body needs different care from your mind and spirit. Much like the mind and spirit need time of quiet and care, movement and gentle care of your body is necessary to aid the integration of body, mind, and spirit. As you care for your body by giving it the movement, food, and rest it needs, it will enhance your healing journey and access to healing.

Movement throughout the day works your muscles and burns calories needed for balance. It is more than our everyday movement that matters, however; it is also important to engage in intentional stretching and gentle care of the body that supports our mind and spiritual work. Exercise is good for your general health, and it has an impact on your healing. The goal for exercise is good balance.

My relationship with exercise connects to self-care and my deep belief systems. My exercise journey has ebbed and flowed between having a great practice to no practice at all at times. My challenge has been centered in belief systems. I needed to get at the root of why I was not able to be consistent with good habits. If you find imbalance, do not be discouraged. Continue to move forward in your healing work and you will see and feel the shifts of progress. My efforts, self-care, and exercise have improved as I continue to work on my healing journey. Prioritizing exercise is an area to pay attention to your healing. If you are excessive about exercise and your body or if it is an area you soon forget, try to become curious about the origins of imbalance or overdoing in your reflection.

There are many ways to move your body. Explore and find movement you enjoy. Below are some examples for you to consider:

- Dancing
- Free movement
- Yoga
- Hiking
- Biking (ebikes count)

Reflect on the following questions about movement:

- What are your thoughts about movement and exercise for your body?
- What movement or exercise do you enjoy the most? What do you love about it?
- What exercise goal(s) do you have moving forward?
- What is your biggest challenge for regular exercise?
- How will you meet exercise challenges in your healing journey?

Food Choices

Food choices are essential in overall wellness. Certain foods deplete the body, while others give us more energy. Everyone's body is different. The critical part of our food choices is connected to our body's needs and wants. You will learn more about your body's needs by getting to know your body, mind, and spirit. Listen to what your body is asking for. As you get to know your body, it will be easier to discern. The body's nutritional needs are what many of us learn in grade school. The point that assisted me in improving my food choices was how this area could connect to the past; food patterns often are learned in early years. They can either be a place for struggle or a place for calm and regulation. Like exercise, the connection to food choices can be linked to past experiences and belief systems. Being curious about any struggle instead of seeing this area as evidence of lack is very important to healing. Be kind to yourself, whether you are obsessive about food choices or you struggle with food choices. Food choices are another area in my life within which the healing work of past harm has enlightened me. As I continued to heal, I intrinsically began to care for myself by making better choices. These new choices became part of who I am.

Try the following suggestions as you work on your relationship with food.

- Balance your eating times and portions
- Decrease processed foods and junk food
- Find veggies you enjoy
- Find fruits you enjoy
- Consume food of high quality
- Choose lean high-quality meats

Reflect on the following questions about food:

- What food choices do you enjoy the most? Why is it so enjoyable?
- What are your thoughts about your relationship with food choices and your body?
- Do you have any goal(s) about food choices moving forward?

Affirmations

Here are some additional affirmations to try to deepen your practice as you move through the levels of healing. As always, I encourage you to create your own supportive and loving affirmations if you are called to do so.

I control my thoughts; my thoughts do not control me.

I desire loving thoughts about myself and others.

*I am worthy of healing and I will fight
for more love and light in my life.*

I have love and compassion for myself.

As I seek truth I will be led to goodness.

Meditation

Set a timer; start at ten or twenty minutes. Find soft soothing music as a backdrop to your quiet time. Do not let your mind tell you that you are not able to meditate for whatever reason. When the thoughts come to defeat your intention, push them away and proceed. These defeating thoughts are part of the trauma protection and part of the unhealed mind that interferes with healing. Start now to notice its messages and gently push them away. You can simply state *not today* or *not now*.

Find a quiet place where you are comfortable and feel safe. Settle yourself into where you are sitting. You can lie down if that is comfortable. Take a deep breath in. Focus your energy and thoughts on your body and the rise and fall of your chest or abdomen. Put all your attention on your breathing.

On the inbreath think *I* and on the outbreath think *am* (repeat until your body sinks into relaxation). Repeat until the timer goes off. Thank your body, wiggle your fingers and limbs, and slowly open your eyes.

The amazing thing about meditation is that, as your body relaxes, the breathing changes and you find yourself at peace. Continue to build this practice until you can feel your body sink into relaxation easier and easier.

In the following section, you will see the same rituals from the previous chapter. The reason these practices repeat is to allow your practice to build and grow and strengthen. It takes time to build what works for your body, mind, and spirit. If you find you would like to build your own affirmations, rituals, and meditation, there will be space at the end of this chapter for you to create.

Rituals

The following rituals will help you build upon the ones you may have already begun to weave into your daily life. Enjoy the depth that these bring.

Morning

When you open your eyes from slumber, take a deep breath in and slowly blow it out. Take a moment of gratitude before you do anything else like grabbing your phone. Center yourself in gratitude. The gratitude can be as simple as *thank you*. Take another deep breath in and slowly blow it out. Have a great day.

Gratitude Ideas

Write a list of gratitudes and use them in your morning awakening. Here are a few examples to get you started:

> *I am grateful for this bed, grateful for my*
> *arms, legs, eyes, and the ability to breathe.*

Midday

Around noon, stop and take a breath. It does not matter what is going on in your life. When you see it is midday, stop and breathe in a positive thought. You are important and worth this brief pause. Think about something that brings you joy (a pet, fun moment, loved one, favorite memory).

Evening

In the evening, before dinner or at bedtime, take a moment to breathe in a positive movement by reading something that is inspirational. This will only take a minute or two. Read an inspirational quote or daily reader with positive messages. Here are a few you can use if they inspire you:

> *I want joy in my life. Joy is more than happi-*
> *ness; it is the bliss of happiness. I find joy in a*

laughing child and a playful puppy. I am joy-
ful and will pull it out of me every day.

Some days my mind wants to wallow in self-pity,
yet I will not let it. I know I have love and light
rather than sadness within. I'm just afraid to come
out. I simply put on a cheerful smile and a good
song, and it eases out of me like cotton candy!

Merry-go-rounds spin and spin and get faster
and faster. The elation is bearable at first and
then it gets to be too much. My goal for my life is
to live in the just-right part of elation by trust-
ing my body, mind, and spirit to hold me.

I know I am at peace when the world and all its
activity stands still and I am one with stillness of my
body, mind, and spirit. My body feels like it's sus-
pended in a fluffy cloud without a worry in the world.

Journal Reflection: Self-Care Tools

In your journal, create personalized affirmations, meditations, and rituals using the examples I've provided throughout the book to guide you.

Chapter Summary

This chapter reviewed the process of moving from trauma response to peace. The Levels of Awareness were reviewed at the beginning of this chapter: Level 1, getting in touch with your body, Level 2, observing mind patterns, and Level 3, breaking free from trauma experiences to move toward peace and freedom as a way of life.

This chapter discussed the thinking patterns that can be a result of trauma or harmful experiences. The lasting residue of harm can color our personalities, relationships, and perceptions.

Introduced in this chapter was the Thinking Map, which is a tool to assist in the examination of experiences more deeply to reveal the undercurrents of trauma and harm that could be influencing you. Deep belief patterns were discussed in this chapter. The belief system is something we want to monitor and change as needed. The chapter reviewed surface, ingrained, and core beliefs. Tools were introduced on how to interrupt and heal all three belief systems.

Lastly, self-care tools were given to continue to build your wellness library more deeply. Additional information was given to deepen your self-care in sleep, exercise, and food choices. Now that you have a deeper understanding and relationship with your body, taking the time to be curious about your thoughts is the next step to integrate what you have learned.

BRINGING IT ALL TOGETHER

This chapter builds upon the previous chapter and refines the connection between body and mind patterns. Various reflective tools will assist in exploring conscious and subconscious thoughts to discover and interrupt negative thinking. Additionally, this chapter will provide self-care tools to continue building a wellness toolbox.

The introduction of connecting to your body occurred in chapters 1 and 2, while chapter 3 discussed the knowledge about trauma and how it shows up in the body. Then, in chapter 4, we introduced the mind patterns and deep belief systems. This chapter will bring together and incorporate the information you have learned and share examples and experiences on using what you have learned to help you discover and reflect on your healing.

To enhance your practice of healing, we must identify subconscious beliefs by looking beyond what we know to be true in our lives. It takes courage to question what we have always known to be our truth. We are examining the fabric of our lives. When you admire a fabric, there are many threads and colors that make up the collection of the whole piece. The reflections and curiosity in this chapter are the examination of the pieces of thread we no longer need.

Using the tools of each level in your life requires moving from body to mind to spirit. The steps to fit it all together are like a puzzle. The consistent relationship with your body may look as varied as meditation walks, massages, or acupuncture. There is no right or wrong way to be in relationship with your body—focus on whatever your body needs to rest and digest life. At this point you may notice things like television shows and media that you had previously watched or participated in are no longer an attraction today. The changes occur subtly. Your mind may have quieted down some; thoughts that used to run through your head without a second thought are now interrupted and replaced by a positive affirmation or positive thought. These subtleties are life-giving steps to the road of freedom. If you are not quite there, more information will be reviewed in this chapter to take your results deeper and to enhance your practice.

Journal Reflection: Level 1 Body Sensations

Using your experience and learning thus far, reflect on the following questions in your journal:

- What have I noticed about my body sensations?
- Where is there a sensation I have not acknowledged before?
- Do I feel in my body when I am uncomfortable or unsettled?

- What does uncomfortable and unsettled look like, feel like, sound like?
- Describe the relationship with your body. What do you love? What do you not like?
- How do you get in touch with what's going on with your body? How do you know your body is uncomfortable, in joy, or content?
- What does your body most enjoy? How do you know?
- How do you celebrate your connection with your body?
- What have you learned about your body that you did not know?
- If you could draw the relationship with your body, what would it look like? Draw a representation in your journal.

Where to Look for Connection

Start looking for connection by examining any experience that continues to linger, such as memories that linger or ideas about yourself that you have noted as facts. If you constantly think or say negative comments about yourself, this is an area to pay attention to. Be curious when you are given positive compliments about yourself. If you find yourself disregarding a compliment or positive comment given to you, pay attention to why you may be uncomfortable accepting positivity. If you think negatively about yourself, pay attention to where those thoughts originate. Anything that is on a low vibration or not positive is a place to be curious about.

What is a low vibration? A low vibration describes the energy of emotional states that are debilitating or do not carry positive feelings. If you have ever walked into a room and did not like the feel of it, the energy in the room was not high. Think about the opposite: if you were in a room that was filled with joy and elation, you could actually feel it!

With that in mind, think about areas of your life that bring a feeling you cannot recognize or that are simply not positive. Begin by doing an examination of your life every day. If you are miffed at someone at work or something bothered you, this is a place to begin. Keep a small notepad with you throughout the day and write down the annoyances that come up. These situations will become the pathway to healing for you. If you can pinpoint areas of your life that need refinement, great! Write them down in your journal and this information will assist you in learning more about yourself.

Areas to consider:

- Romantic relationships (spouse, partners, long and short term)
- Emotional highs or lows
- Family narratives about you
- Food
- Exercise
- Sexual health
- Siblings/children

Finding Calm: Jan's Story

Jan's story is a wonderful example of how it looks to move through the levels of healing and ultimately find calm in the body and mind.

Jan was raised in an upper middle-class family. Her family loved jokes and pranks. They saw it as a form of connection. As a child Jan was often frightened by her mother jumping out from around a corner. Her mother thought it was fun and funny. In addition, her mother had mood swings and would often fly off the handle with loud outbursts or screaming, throwing things, and having tantrums directed at her or other family members. As an adult Jan was easily startled, nervous, and did not like loud sounds. Jan had problems at work with people she described as overbearing and aggressive.

To process the relationship between her and her scary boss, Jan began to seek support. Although meditation was not comfortable for Jan, she was willing to give walking meditation a try (body connection, Level 1). She preferred walking in nature to calm her mind and body. Jan noticed the thoughts that often ran through her mind and made her scared or anxious. The Critic Mind was strong and constantly informed Jan she was not doing it right. Jan used the Thinking Map to help her interrupt the Critic Mind and bring her more peace (mind patterns, Level 2).

After keeping a log of her negative thinking for a few days, Jan used the Thinking Map to understand more about herself (interrupting mind patterns). Jan found that her boss reminded her of her mother. She did not realize the connection. Jan carried her family's prank and unpredictability with her into adulthood. She was finally ready to let those things go (breaking free and reflective tools, Level 3). Through acknowledgment of the past, using the Thinking Map, Jan was able to be curious and let go of some of the energy that was distorting *her perceptions. She used forgiveness and embodied art drawings to let go of the energy around unpredictable behavior. Through work on creating new belief systems and rewriting the narrative, Jan was able to move into a successful role at work.*

It is not surprising that after working on the body-brain connection, examination of explicit and implicit memories and thinking patterns can be interrupted, and rewriting the narrative can lead to spiritual growth. By Jan making space for her body to communicate with her, she was able to make room in her mind to allow for more peace, remove unwanted belief systems, and rewrite harms to embody new energy. How could it not? Nothing was standing in the way of her authentic self.

We have reviewed the ingredients and now it is time to put everything together for a system of healing and peace.

Exploring Body Connections

When I began to connect to my body, I worked on the things I had always worked on: diet and exercise. At the time, I believed I lacked willpower, which is why I struggled with my body's health. I did not consider the harm I had lived through and how it had left a mark on my body, mind, and spirit. The first part of getting to know my body started with what I knew about my experiences. Although I wanted to pull down the shades on all the harmful experiences in my life, I had to acknowledge that each happened. By simply recognizing them, I embodied my power to heal them.

First let's acknowledge anything that has occurred to your body that may be hindering your growth in any way. You may have already worked on this in previous chapters. In your journal, list anything else that comes to mind.

I experienced physical, sexual, and emotional harm, which has left a mark on how I interacted with and understood my body and the world. My first focus was to unlearn the messages I was listening to and what my body was telling me.

- What is the relationship with your understanding of what your body is telling you?
- Do you spend quiet time every day? What messages does your body tell you? Are you listening to your body messages?

In my efforts, I focused on massages, rest, sleep, movement, exercise, diet, food choices, and eating habits. While I was taking these actions, I began meditating to quiet my mind. My thoughts did not support my wellness or self-care. My thoughts cycled on ways I was doing it wrong or how I could improve. It was a struggle at first and meditation gave me the first inroad toward peace.

- What actions have you taken to take care of your body?
- Is your mind supporting your efforts, and if so, how? If not, how?

My focus on my care of my body began with monitoring my sleep. I got an app that tracked the quality of my sleep. I began exercising by taking walks in nature.

- What steps have you taken to connect to your body?
- What steps have you taken for better sleep?
- What steps have you taken for exercise and diet?

Exploring Mind Patterns

Our mind has a life of its own. I do not have control over my thoughts. I was shocked when thoughts entered my mind that I did not like or want. I was sure it originated from me, and I am here to tell you, that is not true. Sometimes the thoughts come from my harmful experiences, generational fear, a story or film, but what I do know is the thoughts that do not bring peace to my body, mind, and spirit are not needed, and I wanted them removed. My thoughts used to be like a locomotive constantly moving and morphing. I thought this was normal, that everyone thought this way. That is not true. My head was not quiet one bit.

As a matter of fact, if you were talking, I would be thinking about what I was going to say next and creating arguments about what you were saying in my head. When I walked away from addiction, my mind settled some. Addiction is a form of altered states and in those alterations thinking can be very chaotic and cycling. Once I detoxed from the alcohol and substances, my life and mind became more serene. Yet, the thoughts would come.

Scenarios of conversation would play out in my head. *I should have said this instead of that*, I would think. So many made-up conversations and scenarios I wasted time having in my mind. I was trying to grasp security and belonging. My head was pretty busy.

I would purposely fantasize about what I wanted. Making up a pretend relationship is much easier in my head than in real life. Fantasizing had been a favorite pastime until one day it caught up with me. I had a crush on my boss, and I think he had one on me too. I thought about us all the time in a relationship. In my mind we were dating. One day I was alone with my boss in a classroom, and I almost kissed him. What was I thinking! I could have lost my job because I was fantasizing so much, I lost touch with reality. That day I stopped that kind of thinking. It scared me and I decided not to lose myself in fantasy. Fantasy can be dangerous. It is in the same family as revenge or getting even.

The chaotic thinking of addiction, obsession, and even fantasy are not serving the highest part of your being. I write these personal examples to cast light on the thinking that sets up unhealthy behavior. This kind of thinking is universal for all kinds of unhealthy thought patterns. Be honest with yourself: Does your thinking at times wander into judgment about yourself or others? Do you find yourself thinking about things that happened in the past or even things that happened years ago? This kind of cycling of the mind is the very thing that needs to be interrupted to bring peace of mind.

I found that I needed to be right here, right now to live in the moment so I was not cycling in my thoughts. I had to work to be in the moment. I wondered why I could not be in the present moment. I always had to be somewhere else. I did not like or love myself because of past harms. I was mentally kicking myself.

The kind of thinking that ruled me the most is what I call tangent thinking. I would be sitting at a stoplight and some phrase would come on the radio. I would think about that phrase or even come up with a critique of the phrase until another thought would pull me away. This kind of thinking could occur at any time, especially when I was bored. Which apparently was a lot. Sometimes really scary thoughts would come into my head. It was always something that could happen to hurt me or those I loved.

Today, I believe these thoughts were generational trauma from the past. In the final chapter of the book, I will further discuss my work with these thoughts. Nevertheless, I was powerless over what came into my mind. How I became the ruler of my thoughts started with me controlling my mind. I said no to thoughts that were scary, sad, frightening, looping, or whatever. If I did not want that thought to rule my mind, I used a mantra to get right of it. I used any means necessary to regain control of my mind. I would say the serenity prayer back-to-back until my mind was clear. I would say another mantra until my head was clear. I would listen to music until my head was clear. I fought back. I now have control over my mind and my mind does not have control over me. Reading this may sound a bit like a cuckoo's nest, but this is how I dealt with my mind in the beginning. I was not going to accept it as it was. Meditation and exercise became the way I paved new pathways in my mind. More and more it became quieter.

Then one day it was quiet for a long time. Do you hear that? It was peaceful. I felt like I had been delivered. This beginning fight was just that. I fought to get my mind back and that was the beginning of a healing journey in my mind. The tools I have suggested are tools after I fought for control. Is there something wrong with me? No. Do I have a diagnosis or some mental illness I did not share? No. I suffered harm over a period of time in childhood and self-induced harm in adulthood, which is very harmful to the body, mind, and spirit. My story could be anyone's story. Suffering harm and rebounding in adulthood to heal the harm and live in peace is possible for anyone.

- What are the thought patterns you are noticing?
- List in your journal the thought patterns that do not bring joy and peace to your life.

Thinking Map Practice

Pick a situation from this week that you did not feel good about. Pick something that bothered you. Use the steps of the thinking map to process your feelings.

Thinking Map Steps

Say a positive intention and affirmation prayer before you begin:

Allow me to see the truth and be a better soul.

Step 1: Pick a situation that has bothered you. The one criterion for the subject is something that rubbed you the wrong way.

Step 2: Write what happened in the situation. Write the bottom line of the situation or what action happened to upset you. This can be difficult to write because most of us have the story or narrative wrapped around the core of the situation. You will get better at this step with practice.

For example: *Bob is always putting me down in work meetings.*

Step 3: Write how you felt about the situation. This can be tricky too because sometimes it is difficult to simply describe the feelings. Use the following list of feelings to guide your exploration here.

Examples of feelings:

- Happy
- Angry
- Surprised
- Ecstatic
- Shy
- Sad
- Disgusted
- Lonely

- Embarrassed
- Empty
- Exhausted
- Overwhelmed
- Afraid
- Smug
- Guilty
- Hopeful
- Jealous
- Confident
- Cautious
- Worried
- Distracted
- Nervous
- Proud
- Frustrated
- Confused
- Depressed
- Ashamed
- Hopeless
- Enraged
- Shocked

Step 4: Write what the deep belief is about yourself. This step can be puzzling until you get used to it. Based on the situation and your feelings, what is the deeper belief about yourself? After you have had time to reflect, pick one of the following descriptions:

HELPLESS

UNACCEPTABLE

DISADVANTAGED

Or

_____ *(you fill in a word)*

HELPLESS means feeling like there is nothing you can do (trapped, powerless).

UNACCEPTABLE means feeling like you are not wanted or deserving (not good enough, thrown away).

DISADVANTAGED means feeling like you are not getting what you deserve (missing out, unfair treatment).

This last question is a difficult one because it is hard to think you have a belief system that is not supporting who you are. Take a deep breath, close your eyes, and the answer will come to you.

Step 5: Was there anything that happened in your early years or in your life that would cause you to believe you are the word you have chosen?

List your answers. Look at what you have written. Ask yourself if these feelings could come from other challenging experiences. Does this situation remind you of unresolved feelings from the past? Your feelings are more likely historical. It is in your past and not what your life is like today. This step removes the subconscious belief from hiding and puts it front and center. In this step, you are shining a light on something untrue.

Step 6: Rewrite the narrative. In this step you communicate that this belief is not true and you write all that is true about you. Write the evidence from your life that proves your hidden belief is false. Cross out this belief (literally) and write a new replacement belief about yourself.

What did you find out about yourself using the Thinking Map tool?

Exploring Deep Belief Systems

It is almost impossible to believe that I would think things about myself that were negative and defeating. Who would want to think about themselves in a way that would cause them harm? No one would want to do that, and it was true. I carried beliefs about myself that harmed my purpose, joy, and quality of life. Like much of my recovery, I had to admit this was true. I wanted to fight back and believe I would never have those beliefs. That was ego. It can be entirely defeating when you are trying to heal and grow. The ego has an uncanny way of turning ideas around to make them about the self. My beliefs got in the way of my growth and wellness. I needed to identify when the ego was projecting a story that would keep me from addressing an issue. That is why this work takes deep intent to believe in yourself and to walk forward. Parts of your thinking may be discouraging you from exploring areas. If you ever need additional assistance, seek a professional to help you. Areas where profound harm has occurred may require additional support to fully heal. The most important thing is to realize that you are perfect, and that inner peace is your goal.

Some psychologists write about our thoughts as if they live outside of us and can be thrown away by self-knowledge. I wish it was that easy, but it has been a process to rid myself of belief systems that are troubling for me. It takes time to identify them, find the origin, and interrupt and dispel the belief. For example, imposter syndrome is the belief you are a fraud; it's an internal anxiousness about being successful. In my opinion, it is a deep belief. I was coaching a person who was more than adequate for the job, but he believed he had imposter syndrome. He felt he did not measure up and put a lot of pressure on himself. One session we had was about him managing his employees. He was nervous about it and was frozen in fear. Using the Thinking Map, we were able to identify in his childhood he was constantly told he could not measure up because of his body size. Situation after situation he shared where his father told him because he was shorter, he could not do what others could do. That information stuck to him, and he had carried it into adulthood and into the job he loved. The deep belief in this story is that he thought he was not capable of his job. We together rewrote the narrative:

I am not capable to do my job.

I am capable of any job. I hold all the necessary learning, skills, and experience to do my job well.

Rewrite the narrative:

I have earned degrees in business and management. I have extensive experience in my field. I am more than capable to provide the expertise to do my job and to assist those who work with me to be their best.

Younger Versions of Yourself

When the belief system is centered on childhood memories, harm, or experiences, it requires more nurturing for the developmental age that has been neglected or harmed. Boni Lonnsburry in her book, *The Map to Our Responsive Universe Where Dreams Really Do Come True*, discusses at length how to engage with versions of yourself at different ages. What occurs in the different stages of growing up is that the feelings are entrenched, and at times, a younger you can show up in your adult life.

Think about a time you have observed an adult behaving childishly in a situation. What happened that made an adult revert to a five-year-old? The younger version of yourself can show up in your adult body especially if struggles mirror an age where unresolved harm has occurred. It feels like your adult body has been transported to a different planet and a version of you, younger you, is in charge of your adult situation. I have experienced this phenomenon, and I am grateful for the healing and insight I have learned from working with Boni Lonnsburry and the work I have put into healing those younger years that have shown up in my adult life. The tools you have learned in this book will work for you in this area too. Be curious about things you say and do and the answers seem to always come. Let me give an example.

My family and I took a winter trip to a National Park a few years ago. It was great. It was very isolated, snowy, and quiet. As we planned each day together, my spouse and I asked our son about his choices and preferences. He got an opportunity to share his thoughts, and we listened. I became moody and irritable during the trip about things my son suggested. I knew something was off because I had no reason to feel this way. I became curious as to what began these feelings. I took out the Thinking Map and did some writing. I found that my ten-year-old self was jealous of the care and love my son was getting. It is true. I was far from ten years old, and because I was willing to be curious about my feelings, I discovered that at ten years old, I must have struggled with how I felt about being heard and feeling like I mattered to my parents. I had no specific memory, but my feelings were strong and spot on. I learned from a fantastic coach to reflect and go back to the age I was struggling with to ask that particular age their needs. Like many things that have worked for me, I thought this was very silly, but I was willing to try it and found it to be a fantastic tool for self-healing. I have used the tool before and know it works well. I found an isolated spot where I could be alone to sit quietly in meditation. Once I was still and my head was quiet, I asked my ten-year-old self if they had any needs. The responses rushed into my thoughts. I wrote them all down.

I want parents who care about what I think.

I want parents who ask my opinion about things.

I want parents to take me on trips that I pick.

I want my interests to be supported.

I want parents who show me love by hugging me and telling me they love me.

I was in awe. All the things that showed up in my writing were how my spouse and I were treating our son. During the trip, I had reverted to a ten-year-old, and I was jealous of the treatment my spouse and I were giving our son. My ten-year-old self's feelings were occurring in my fifty-year-old body. How can that even be true?

The next step in my journaling was to ensure and care for my ten-year-old self. I did that by rewriting the narrative. I assured my ten-year-old self that they would get all they wanted and that I, the adult me, would provide their wishes. I then asked them in writing to stay in the ten-year-old realm. I would now take care of them, and as an adult, I was okay. I cannot even begin to express how potent this activity was. I am so grateful I was willing to try it.

During my life, a younger self will show up in my psyche, emotions, and actions to protect me from past harm or stand up for me. By knowing my body, reflecting on my thinking, and exploring curiosity, I can interrupt and heal the past. The healing actions I take transform energy that was once a protection and put it back into my body as good positive energy. Imagine situation after situation being resolved and healed. Because of the healing, I have a newfound awareness of similar situations that do not have the same power over me because of the healing that has taken place. How amazing is that? Using these tools slowly transformed my body, mind, and spirit.

Healing through Energy Medicine

Energy medicine focuses on the energy in our bodies. We have energy centers that take in information and output information. I had not heard of energy medicine until I began teaching Strategies for Trauma Awareness and Resilience. My coteacher and friend mentioned energy medicine to me as a form of healing. Yeah, right, I thought to myself. I did not believe her; I believed it was mumbo jumbo. Although I thought it was very nice that my friend Katie believed in this energy medicine, I did not know it was real. While teaching our course together, my heart rate spiked to 127. I was wearing a tracking device and noticed on a break that my heart rate was too high. I walked over to my friend and told her something was wrong with me.

My heart was racing. Katie immediately closed her eyes and held her hands up before me. I was reticent, and as flippant as I had been in the past about energy medicine not being natural, I humbly stood still. Katie opened her eyes and informed me that my energetic boundaries were torn. What are energetic boundaries? I asked her why this had happened to me. Katie shared with me that I am a caring person, and the participants in the course are needy. I was trying to meet their needs, and it damaged my energetic boundaries. I still did not understand, but my friend lowered my heart rate three times during the day. As I lay in bed that night, I knew energy medicine was real because I had witnessed it.

The next day, my heart rate was still racing off and on. I did not know how to control it. I asked Katie what I should do over the weekend as we would not be together, and I did not know how to control it myself. She tossed the book *Energetic Boundaries* by Cyndi Dale on the table before me. I picked up the large book and wondered what I would do with it. I had not heard of Cyndi Dale, an internationally renowned author, speaker, healer, and business consultant. I found a short audiobook, *Healing Through the Chakras* by Cyndi Dale, and learned to control my racing heart independently in a few hours. This was my introduction to energy medicine.

Through my studies, I learned that energy is in everything and everywhere. My body has seven primary energy centers called chakras. These chakras take in energy and can affect my life experiences. I could carry a spot or injury on my chakra based on the harm I experienced. This information got my attention. I was working on removing harm in my body, mind, and spirit, and there was an area of my body I had not paid attention to or knew carried this harm too. I became a student of energy medicine. I began to learn all I could and practiced clearing my chakras and energy of harm.

I began healing my energy issues through guided meditation by Cyndi Dale in her audiobooks. These worked for me. I learned about energy medicine and used the tools in the books to heal my energy. I began to see results in my practices.

One profound energy healing I experienced was in the area of sexual abuse. As a four-year-old, I was sexually molested by an older cousin who was twelve years old. I was sure I was over this harm, yet when I began to follow a guided meditation for healing to remove any scars on my chakras, I found myself at the scene of this abuse. I was unhappy to be back on the scene and continued to follow the meditation, although I did not want to. I experienced compassion and forgiveness for my cousin and myself in the meditation. When the meditation was over, I was surprised I could feel a sense of freedom. I had healed something I didn't even know I was still carrying.

I had another healing in this area that surprised me. I was exploring my energy in the area of money and did a similar exploration meditation and found myself back at the scene of the sexual abuse when I was four years old. One way my cousin lured me into isolation was with a gum I liked. In my meditation, I reconciled the untruth that I was getting paid for my abuse. I had no idea how that subconscious thought came to be. Subconsciously, I believed that I was being paid with gum somehow. Therefore, my relationship with money had an unhealthy energy around it. That was a lie. I was a child. I was not paid; my cousin manipulated me. The negative energy around money was cleared, and more good energy came into my body.

I share this to illustrate the importance of energy medicine. You may not have had the exact experiences I had, but you may be able to shed light on a subconscious belief, action, or system that is not working for your benefit.

The seven chakra energy centers in your body are located at different parts of your body.

Understanding the Chakras

Cyndi Dale's book *New Chakra Healing* is an encyclopedia of information about chakras. The following is a snapshot of information about chakras using this text as a resource. The root chakra is the first chakra; it gives us a foundation for who we are. If we feel challenged, the root chakra gives us the strength to persevere. The root chakra is vital to living. The yang of the root chakra is your projection and survival in the world, and the yin is associated with our will to live and how we receive assistance in life. Issues with addiction, family and sexual dysfunction, childhood abuse, money, food, housing, and so on can be associated with this chakra. If you use chromatic notes for chakra balancing, Middle C is the note for the first chakra.

The sacral chakra is the second chakra; it governs energy relating to the inner and outer world, and how we feel or express ourselves is located in the second chakra. Its color is orange. Creative and emotional expression is part of the second chakra. The yang is an expression of the feelings of others, and the yin involves perceiving other feelings by deciphering how you feel about the information perceived. Problems in childhood, such as creative block and codependency, can be related to the second chakra. If you use chromatic notes for chakra balancing, D is the note for the second chakra.

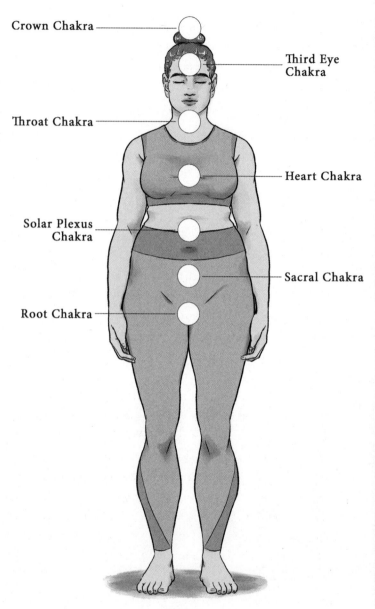

Crown Chakra

Third Eye Chakra

Throat Chakra

Heart Chakra

Solar Plexus Chakra

Sacral Chakra

Root Chakra

Chakras

The solar plexus chakra is the third chakra; it is where self-control—the place of knowingness, confidence, and the ability to feel in control of life—lies. Its color is yellow. The yang interprets how one sees oneself in the world, and the yin perceives the opinions and judgments of the world and others. Problems with digestion, weight, confusion, and power issues can be related to the third chakra. If you use chromatic notes for chakra balancing, E is the note for the third chakra.

The heart is the fourth chakra, the center of the body, and the connection for spiritual and divine energy. Its color is green. The yang is associated with relations to others and our gifts to the universe, and the yin is related to relations with others and what we receive from the universe. Problems with the heart, blood pressure, lung issues, codependency, and caretaking can be associated with this chakra. If you use chromatic notes for chakra balancing, F is the note for the fourth chakra.

The throat chakra is the fifth chakra; it centers on communication, manifesting, and protecting the self. Its color is sky blue. The yang is associated with expressing and voicing the truth, and the yin receives guidance—problems with the throat, jaw, victimhood, or under- or overresponsibility. If you use chromatic notes for chakra balancing, G is the note for the fifth chakra.

The third eye is the sixth chakra; it governs perception, awareness, and spiritual communication. Its color is purple. The yang is associated with the ability to see, plan, and measure the future. The yin is associated with self-image and perception. Problems with headaches, looking ahead, and self-image may be centered in this chakra. If you use chromatic notes for chakra balancing, B is the note for the fifth chakra.

Lastly, the crown chakra represents spiritual connection and transformation. It's the higher knowing center and center for divinity. The yang represents living with a divine purpose, and the yin is associated with energies to fuel our spiritual selves. Problems with understanding yourself and your purpose may be related to this chakra. If you use chromatic notes for chakra balancing, High C is the note for the seventh chakra.

As you can see, the energy centers are essential to healing. Knowing about each one and what it represents can assist in focusing on areas that require healing and care. Additional resources are in the back of the book.

An example of how a chakra can help healing is when I was following a guided meditation to clear my throat chakra. During the meditation, I felt like I was in a cave with little room to move. I was surprised by that feeling. I thought I spoke up for myself and advocated clearly, but my throat chakra was constricted. After the meditation, I did some reflective writing and found that my constriction was related to a situation that happened to me when I was very young. My father physically punished me for lying, and I was telling the truth. I was surprised that this harm was revealed; I was so young. I used the tool of forgiveness and the meditation of shame for this harm.

There were two things I needed to do for these feelings and energy. One is I need to return the shame given to me in the harm. I learned that shame is a deficient energy and needs to be discarded; it must be given to the person who gave it to you. I did this through meditation. In the meditation, I took a trusted person with me (a spiritual guide) and visited the house of shame. In my meditation, it is a raggedy wooden shack. I travel in a dark forest, through brush and bushes and trees, up and down hills until I see the wooden shack, and with courage, I enter and find the room with the people or person who harmed me. At first, I watched the scene before me and watched the harm happen. It is hard to watch. After I observed the harm, the adult me spoke up for myself and handed the shame back to the person who gave it to me through harm. Next, in the meditation, I leave and go back through the forest, brush, bushes, and trees to the safe place. I sat and enjoyed my special place of healing, with a waterfall and soothing water on a fabulous beach. My throat chakra became free.

- What do you know about chakras?
- Is there a part of your body that is constantly aching or in pain?
- What chakras do you feel need healing?
- What chakras are filled with joy and happiness?

Muscle Testing to Support Healing

Our bodies interpret our experiences through feelings consciously and unconsciously. Most of us focus on the conscious level, but few realize what occurs on the unconscious level. The saying that the "body knows" is true. How can we possibly know what our body desires?

In 1964, a chiropractor named Dr. Goodheart correlated muscles' negative and positive responses. He found that the corresponding muscle was tight if one muscle was weak.

Dr. Goodheart discovered that the body could tell what was good or bad through muscle communication. His discovery was the beginning of what is known today as muscle testing.

In 1970, Dr. John Diamond continued Dr. Goodheart's discovery in the book *Your Body Doesn't Lie.* Dr. Diamond found that a muscle could be strong or weak when given positive or negative information. Dr. Diamond used the vibration of music, pictures, symbols, and food to test the body's communication. He was able to positively show the body's sense of knowing what is good and what is bad. This knowledge base is called specialized kinesiology.

This field is known as specialized kinesiology, a form of energy medicine that uses muscle testing to identify structural, muscular, chemical, emotional, and mental issues. The idea behind muscle testing is that your body knows what is best. You can navigate barriers when you bypass the ego mind and use the body as a communication tool. To some, this may be new information. Muscle testing as a form of communication can assist you in your healing journey. Specialized kinesiology professionals include a wide range of professions, including educators, chiropractors, athletes, medical doctors, acupuncturists, and physical therapists.

Muscle testing can assist each of us in healing and communicating with our bodies. Imagine using your body's responses to discover past harm from your life or lifetimes ago. You want to understand the vibration of trauma responses within you and interrupt the fright and anxiety.

Muscle testing can help identify hidden feelings.

My favorite resource for muscle testing is *Every Body's Truth, Muscle Testing for the Masses*, written by Rev. Dr. AdaRA L. Walton, a Doctor of Naturopathy who holds a PhD in Natural Health and is a Reiki Master, Shaman, and Spiritual Medium. In her book, Rev. Dr. AdaRA L. Walton chronicles many topics, including balancing, nutrition, and muscle testing.

Using muscle testing could help you know what your body wants and desires. I learned muscle testing from Rev. Dr. AdaRA, and I use it to help me with unconscious feelings in my body. This tool can be used and learned to assist in your healing journey.

To understand how muscle testing works, accepting that your body is energy is essential. Your body has energy centers, the chakras, meridians, and more. The meridians are invisible highways of energy running positively and negatively through your body. Simply put, the meridians flow from the earth-yin or the sun-yang. You have positive chi or balance and harmony when everything is running well. When things are blocked or stagnant, your chi is constricted. The focus is to remove what is blocking your balance and preventing your harmony. Many things can block your chi, from diet to the environment.

Can You Do Muscle Testing?

I learned muscle testing from a spiritual mentor teacher and from studying independently. I have learned that it is important to be neutral about what you are asking/stating to your body and to always begin by putting yourself in a protected space or the highest light or love. I use the White Light Prayer to start my sessions.

> *In the name of Source (universe, God, I am, etc.),*
> *I ask for the highest white light and vibration*
> *on the right of me and the left of me, all around*
> *me and through me, over my head and under*
> *my feet in all spaces known and unknown.*

*Let there be no interference right here, right
now, and so it is in the name of Source.*

This general covering of protection is what I use universally for all spiritual work and connections to the body. Make the prayer work for you. The important part is to keep the vibrations of the words and your intentions in the highest and most favorable light.

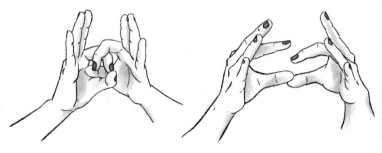

Muscle Testing
Referenced from Rev. Dr. AdaRA L. Walton.

For self-testing, you will ask your body yes-no questions or make statements. If a subject/issue is too deeply rooted, you may be unable to work on it alone. Begin slowly to get to know your body and start by asking questions or making statements about things that are not high stakes. If you are not comfortable with self-testing, it is okay. Do not try to force it; your body and mind know your heart. If you are willing to walk forward, become as neutral as possible.

Once you have said your prayer, you will be learning one example of muscle self-testing. There are other ways of self-testing. Look at the picture of the Linked Ring self-testing.

1. Using your thumb and second finger of both hands, link them together. Tell your body to show you a yes then pull your fingers. The fingers on both hands will stay strong/lock together; this is a yes.

2. Then tell your body to show you a no. Link the fingers of both hands together again and pull. The fingers on both hands will give way or weaken/unlock. This is a no. You *must practice* this process repeatedly a few times before making a statement/asking a question. It's suggested that you take a question and make it into a statement—it's easier for the body to respond/answer yes or no. The body can't answer open-ended questions; it will respond to statements.

Once you've done a few practice questions, take a deep breath and clear your mind. Make a statement with something low stakes, like the statement below.

Broccoli is a good food for me today.

Remember, if your fingers continue to lock or remain strong, that is a yes. If your fingers break away, that is an unlock, muscle is weak, and that is a no.

You hold all the power you need to heal. Use your new tool and get to know your body bit by bit. Take it slow and believe in the most awesome version of yourself. Be clear and have confidence! Practice, practice, practice.

Healing through Connecting to Your Spirit Self

Everyone comes from different places, backgrounds, and belief systems. The most powerful part of my connection to my spiritual self is that I can see and experience my life in a new and enlightened way. The first step was removing the debris between me and my spiritual self. The second step was establishing my willingness and faith to be touched by spirit. For spiritual connection to occur, I had to be ready, remove barriers, shed worldly issues, and raise my vibrational ability to receive. Raising vibrational ability is a by-product of removing past harms—it's a by-product of working your way through the levels of healing. By clearing energetic patterns and challenges, you can meet your spiritual self and connect to higher vibrational support in the spirit world.

There is work that needs to happen to get to that point. To authentically make strides takes commitment to sit in quiet time or the power of your light under the highest light and protection prayer. I began by sitting several times daily, reading the primer *How to Meet and Work with Spirit Guides* by Ted Andrews, an internationally recognized author, teacher, mystic, and master storyteller in the shamanic tradition, and working with a well-versed spiritual teacher. All these tools came to me before I realized what was happening. I said yes every step of the way! Spiritual development does not occur in isolation. Work with others on the same path you are embarking on. Support is suggested throughout this book, and this topic is no different. The universe can put the right people in your life at the right time.

"As above, so below" is a phrase my spiritual mentor reminds me of. There are negative spirits as well as positive ones. It is a fact that is important when learning about spirituality. Your abundance in the spirit world requires an acknowledgment of such factors. This information is not shared to scare you or prevent you from connecting with spiritual relationships that will enhance your life. In his book, Ted Andrews states, "We do not hide in our homes because we have heard there are bad people in the world. We decide who to allow in our lives, physical and spiritual. We control it."[5]

My connection in the spirit world has assisted me in growing in the likeness of my creator, walking on the path of my service, and encouraging and loving me through my walk on Earth. I never walk alone. There is so much fulfillment in spiritual connection. There is mysticism, wonder, inspiration, creativity, the spirit power of the animal world, master teachers, fairy kingdoms, angelic protection, expansive knowledge, and guidance for us in our lives. I have been in contact with friends and relatives who live in the spirit world. I am guided by spiritual beings who have lived on Earth. I am mystified by the world's great wonders on the earth plane and beyond. These wonders are available to you too.

To walk this path, clear the blemishes and marks of harm in your life. Give yourself the gift of sitting still to connect to your higher self. Find a group of like-minded spiritual seekers and a mentor, or be open to them finding you. Hold on to your seat because the ride is a mystical feat of joy and bliss!

What are your experiences with the world of spirit?

My Experience with Spirituality

My journey through the world of spirituality began in childhood when I connected to the outdoors on my grandfather's farm. For

---

5. Andrews, *How to Meet and Work with Spirit Guides.*

me, the connection to nature was my first love, although I did not have a name for it. What I thought was spirituality was the religion I grew up in, Southern Baptist. My grandfather was the Deacon in a church in rural Arkansas, and my grandmother was a Church Mother. The Deacons led the service with the pastor, and the Church Mothers were elderly churchwomen who sat in the front row. I spent the summers with my grandparents, and this is the church I remember most. Church was scary at times because I did not know what was happening. Sometimes, people would yell or shout, and I was told this was the Holy Spirit. The Holy Spirit was good, but it did not look good at all. The preacher would yell loudly and teach the lesson. No matter what he said, people agreed. I was confused by it, but the singing was beautiful, and my heart was complete when the music played. If the Baptist Church was the answer to how I would connect to spirit, I was not interested.

When I was in my late twenties, I was struck sober. One day, I was drinking and using, and the next day, I had a spiritual experience that changed my life forever: a white light experience. I was suddenly alert to what was going on in my life. I was so grateful. I could suddenly see in color. I could see the roses and the blue sky and cherish the beauty of being alive. This event in my life was the beginning of a spiritual way of looking at the world. Something saved me and changed my perception and actions. I could feel what I describe as the spirit of the universe. My experience helped me connect spiritually. It was not organized religion that brought me the connection with the spirit world.

What it felt like was a chill or overly happy feeling, especially when I sang or listened to music. I believed there was something greater than me, and I was delighted with that. I knew right from wrong and had lived close to darkness when I was drinking. I would have never imagined there was more. The growth, healing, and love of myself expanded my ability to see and know realms of spiritual awareness. When I made room for more good in my life by removing harm and resentment, a light that I cannot explain or comprehend moved into me. The work of healing made me closer to the creator or universe. Initially, conceptualizing it was hard, but the feelings, messages, and guidance were undeniable.

This relationship with the spirit world, unseen friends, angels, guidance, and ancestors is extraordinary. Like most things, one of my first spiritual experiences came unexpectedly. A dear friend died suddenly, and I was devastated. The week before, I felt like something was going to happen; someone was going to die. I could not shake the feeling. It was a sad day to know my dear friend had died suddenly. After hearing the news earlier in the week, I woke up at night and saw someone standing at the end of the bed. I thought it was my spouse. Once I blinked a few times, the figure took off fast and out of the room. Wow, where is my spouse going so fast? I thought. Then I reached over in bed, and my spouse and our youngest son were there. Our boy had climbed into our bed during the night. Who was the visitor? Was it my dear friend?

I sought the answer from a trusted energy medicine practitioner. I listened to the suggestions to ground myself, cover myself in the highest light, and ask in writing about my friend who had passed. Following the directions, I asked my friend if she was in my room, and I received a message from my friend in the spirit world. The words came into my head and onto the paper. It was my first spiritual writing message from the spirit world. That was the beginning of my close connection with the spirit world. It is a loving, wonderful connection, and I know if I had not done the work to remove the debris of harm, I would not have experienced this wonderful gift. It is here for all of us.

Ask yourself what stands between you and your spiritual self. An amazing spiritualist master teacher leads me, and I am overjoyed by the care and love I receive daily from my unseen guides. These experiences are available to us all. Clear the path, and great lessons will find you.

Forgiveness as a Door to Deeper Spiritual Connection

To open ourselves up to a higher vibrational state of being and a deeper connection with our spiritual self, we must specifically work through the process of forgiveness. Forgiveness is for the person forgiving, not for those who have harmed. I thought it was enough that I did not want to choke people for hurting me. That is not enough, I found. I needed to forgive for my better well-being and care. The energy of the harm lingered in my energy centers and belief systems. I needed to be ready to forgive them and forgive myself for my ill feelings toward them. This form of forgiveness was challenging. I got to a place where I wanted to be free more than I wanted to hate them for being so cruel to me. I choose to forgive in conjunction with the work mentioned in this chapter.

My awareness came from a conversation I had with both of my parents. While on speakerphone, my dad suggested I talk to his mother, who had passed away. This suggestion was odd as my parents do not connect to the spirit world. Before I could stop myself, I said, "Your mother was not nice in this life, and she probably is not nice in the next!" Whoops. I could not believe I'd even said that. It had flown out of my mouth, and before I knew it, I was off the phone and calling my spiritual teacher. I will never forget the words she said to me in that call.

You are digging a grave for yourself to jump in.

Those words and imagery made me stop and listen. Was I still resentful of my dad's mother for being unkind to us when I was growing up? I always figured she was mean to me because my dad was not my biological father. She was often unhappy, and all these years later, I was holding it against her. My mentor told me that maybe my grandmother wanted to see me. What?

Please take one of your guides to cross
the bridge and see what she wants.

I am a student who listens. I asked one of my guides to take me across the bridge to see my grandmother. My grandmother appeared and asked for my forgiveness. She apologized for being unkind to me and said she had learned many things in the spirit world. She wondered if I would forgive her. I was in tears. I had been holding on to old stuff when my grandmother in the spirit world worked on improving herself. With tears in my eyes, I said of course, I forgave her and asked for her forgiveness for the resentment and harshness I had expressed over the years. We forgave each other. I also forgave myself for the way I'd behaved. After this experience, I began to practice regular forgiveness.

I went back through my life and forgave each harm I could think of—the other person and myself—the foundation of spiritual truth. I no longer needed to hang on to the harm. I could release it and, therefore, release myself to more profound enlightenment.

Who is on your forgiveness list?

Journal Reflection: Levels of Healing

Use the prompts below to capture your reflections about the previous section in your journal. These guiding prompts are provided to assist you in this reflection process.

- Reflect on your experience with Level 1: Body Sensations.
- Reflect on your experience with Level 2: Mind Patterns.
- Reflect on your experience with Level 3: Reflective Tools and Positive Connection to Body, Mind, and Spirit.

Self-Care Tools: Integrating Mind, Body, and Spirit

Explore these self-care tools as you continue to build on and deepen your practice and learn how to integrate your mind, body, and spirit for ultimate healing.

Embodiment Activities

Our bodies have amazing ways to connect to our souls. Everyone is not the same, nor do they need the same kind of tools and support. Getting to know your body by finding the light within is the goal of this exploration. An important factor is to continue to seek and say yes to what calls to you. Activities that may support your body's journey are embodied activities. Using your senses, you can explore the relationship with your body. Embodiment is the heightened awareness and connection to your body and mind and spirit through your senses. Be curious about what your body would like to explore.

Nothing gets the body moving like dancing. An awesome song can release your mind and body into another dimension. If you want to feel the movement in a group, look for fitness, free movement, and ecstatic dance activities near you.

Embodied voice work was pioneered by New York University professor Lisa Sokolov. Embodied voice work is feeling your voice. It is a connection to your voice, along with listening and forming an energy connection with other voices. Singing at home in the kitchen works too! The joy of singing without an agenda or perfectionism feels very good.

Sand tray is the kinesthetic use of sand and figures to express feelings and emotions. Sand tray is a process that assists you in work through areas of healing consciously and unconsciously. A tray of sand can be a soothing sensation to feel with your hands. The movement of different textures, colors, and molding of sand can be soothing and relaxing. Engaging in a sand tray with both hands allows communication between the left and right hemispheres, which is referred to as neural integration. The sand tray can unearth experiences, implicit memories, and trauma through attuned relationships and safety. If you find yourself enjoying the sand, it may mean that it's an effective way to connect to yourself. The sand tray practice uses a variety of figurines to communicate your feelings and thoughts. Figurines generally represent a wide area of protective, creative, emotional release and combative figures. Using the figures, focus on an area of healing; place them in the sand. If you move on to use figures to express your emotions or feelings, be sure to get some guidance and support. Sand tray is not meant to be used alone in isolation.

Visualization can be used as a tool to relax, change moods, and project healing and light. Visualization is the ability to see in your mind's eye what you desire. Imagine a beautiful beach, clear water, and nice breeze. See yourself sitting and enjoying the perfect weather. The water comes into shore and gently goes out to the ocean. Visualization can also be used by viewing videos of nature scenes and soft calming music.

Grounding is a way to center your body, mind, and spirit. Walking barefoot on the grass, dirt, or sand is a form of grounding yourself into the earth. Another form of grounding is rubbing your feet on the floor and using your intent to push energy into the floor down onto the earth then pulling new energy from the floor up into your body. Contracting and constricting your muscles is a form of grounding your body. To do this, take a deep breath and tighten all muscles by pulling your arms inward and tightening your legs then releasing all of them at once. This tightening and release is soothing and takes practice. Explore and seek what works for your body, mind, and spirit.

Meditation is a form of reset at any time. Find mantras, sayings, phrases, or music that can assist you in pausing in the time of need. Using the words *so calm* over and over again is a useful tool for resetting. Any phrase of comfort will assist you in providing your body, mind, and spirit with loving support.

Utilizing creativity and art is a way to access all there is, the universe. Tap into any and all creative interests. Do not let your internal critic diminish your light. Being creative is about the process, not the product. Let yourself experience the joy and bliss of creative activities while you are healing your body, mind, and spirit.

What will you commit to using to support your body?

Quiet Time

Take quiet time daily. Try to pause at least three times a day if you can (morning, noon, and evening). Take a moment to take a mental break and be creative. Pick a guided meditation and listen to it whether you can sit down or not. Listen to a favorite inspirational song.

Nature Walks

Take a walk in nature; breathe in the trees, flowers, and blue sky. It does not matter how much nature is around; get out in it and enjoy it. Clear your mind as you stroll and look at all there is as your body relaxes.

Yoga

Yoga is a mental and spiritual practice originated in ancient India. Yoga practices strengthen balance and flexibility. Yoga is a great way to connect to your body. It can be a challenge, and like everything else, take it slow.

Music as Meditation

Music is a great way to take a breath and meditate on inspirational words. Make a list of your most inspirational and good-energy songs.

Positive Self-Talk

Use positive self-talk throughout the day. Anytime there is a negative thought that runs through your mind, have a phrase or positive thoughts ready to go. Use positive thoughts to replace any imaginings, thoughts, or memories that are not positive.

Recording and Listening Practice

This is a practice that was developed by Zen Buddhist monk Cheri Huber. In the practice, you record yourself talking on topics and then listen back to the recording without straying away from the listening. The goal is to listen to your recording at least three times completely focused without straying thoughts. I love this practice. I had no idea how much my thinking strayed away from focusing.

I am going to recommend you begin to write a love letter to yourself. After you write the letter, record yourself reading it and listen to the recording three times with complete focus. If your mind strays from the recording, start over.

Affirmations

Let's visit some affirmations that flow through all three levels of healing.

Level 1

I am connected to my body.
I listen to my body's communication to me.
I want to heal my body, mind, and spirit.

Level 2

I control my mind.
My thoughts are loving, kind, and peaceful.

Level 3

I am worthy of love and care.
I love and care for my body, mind, and spirit.
I am a thoughtful and loving person.
I am proud of myself.

I feel at peace.
I am courageously healing.

Meditations

We are going to explore two different meditations to expand your practice. With each meditation, begin with the White Light Prayer.

White Light Prayer

In the name of Source (universe, God, I am, etc.),
I ask for the highest white light and vibration
on the right of me and the left of me, all around
me and through me, over my head and under
my feet in all spaces known and unknown.

Let there be no interference right here, right
now, and so it is in the name of Source.

Chakra Meditation

Begin with the White Light Prayer, and then find a comfortable place and gently close your eyes.

Take time to settle yourself and breathe deeply. You need to get to a state of calm. When you are calm in your mind, body, and spirit, open the door to your subconscious. You can visualize it as a door; open it and walk in. You will immediately feel like you are in complete darkness as you travel through a tunnel. Do not be afraid. Call on Source to be closer to you. Let yourself go. When you stop traveling through the tunnel, you will find yourself at the place and time you need to address. You will travel to a day and time that has impacted your _____ (choose chakra) or foundation. Continue to breathe peacefully and consistently. The purpose of your journey is to witness and bring light unto this situation to move the harmful energy from this place. As an observer, witness what happened that your body has held on to. Are you willing to resolve this issue right now?

Answer yes, no, or not right now.

If you chose not right now, say the following: I love myself enough to provide care for all my energy systems. I will come back to this time and place for healing.

If you answer no, say the following: I am not ready today and I intend to be ready to provide the care I need. I love myself enough to revisit this memory.

If you answer yes, take a deep breath and review the scene that left a mark on your energy center. After observing, take another deep breath and look at each soul involved. What happened to the others who were involved? How did they get to this place and time? What can their story be? Take a deep breath and hold it. Slowly let it go. Are you ready to let this situation and all the energy around it go? Are you ready to provide the love, care, and nourishment you need to move forward? Are you ready to release all involved, including yourself? If yes, watch each individual turning into a shining bright light and slowly rise up and out of sight. Watch until you cannot see anything. Take a deep breath and slowly blow it out. Turn away and travel back. Come back to awareness slowly. Thank your spiritual guidance Source.

This meditation is a beginning for your healing journey. You may need additional support; check the Wellness Tool Kit to review tools introduced in the book.

Body Connection Meditation

Now let's do a meditation to connect to the body and reflect on what you have experienced so far. Through this meditation, you will practice and get to know yourself and your body better. The more you know the peace within, the more you can prepare yourself to listen to your body. During the meditation, pay attention to sensations that arise.

Begin this meditation by reciting the White Light Prayer on page 169.

Take a deep breath in. Breathe in deeply and breathe out slowly. Concentrate on the rise and fall of your chest or abdomen for several minutes. Tell your body to relax. Focus on the top of your head and imagine warm soothing water pouring over your body.

Start at the top of your head and ask your body to relax and pause for a few minutes as you feel your body sinking into a relaxed state.

Ask the back of your neck to relax and pause for a few minutes as you feel your body sinking into a relaxed state.

Move on to your shoulders; pause for a few minutes as you feel your body sinking into a relaxed state.

Ask your neck to relax; pause for a few minutes as you feel your body sinking into a relaxed state.

Ask your chest to relax; pause for a few minutes as you feel your body sinking into a relaxed state.

Ask your arms to relax; pause for a few minutes as you feel your body sinking into a relaxed state.

Ask your torso to relax; pause for a few minutes as you feel your body sinking into a relaxed state.

Ask your elbows to relax; pause for a few minutes as you feel your body sinking into a relaxed state.

Ask your fingers to relax; pause for a few minutes as you feel your body sinking into a relaxed state.

Ask your hips to relax; pause for a few minutes as you feel your body sinking into a relaxed state.

Ask your backside to relax; pause for a few minutes as you feel your body sinking into a relaxed state.

Ask your thighs to relax; pause for a few minutes as you feel your body sinking into a relaxed state.

Ask your knees to relax; pause for a few minutes as you feel your body sinking into a relaxed state.

Ask your feet, toes, and bottom of your feet to relax.

Stay in this state for as long as comfortable. When you are ready, take a deep breath in and hold it for a few seconds and slowly let your breath out. Take another deep breath in and hold it for a few seconds and slowly let your breath out. Take one more deep breath in and hold it for a few seconds and slowly let your breath out. Slowly come back by wiggling your fingers and your limbs and slowly opening your eyes.

Rituals

Continue deepening your daily ritual practice.

Morning

Upon waking, take a deep breath and set your intention about the day before you get up.

I am capable and calm.

I am capable and calm.

I am capable and calm.

When you put your feet on the ground, take another deep breath. Focus on pulling energy from the crown of your head down your body and out the soles of your feet to the floor down into the earth. Take another deep breath and pull new fresh energy from the earth up through your feet, up your body, up to the crown of your head. Take your time to feel the power of the energy rise through your body.

Noon

Pause at noon and review your affirmation for the day.

I am capable and calm.

I am capable and calm.

I am capable and calm.

If you can make space, take time for a small meditation or peaceful movement.

Evening

Thank you, Mother Earth, for my daily wanderings.

Bring peace to my slumber and joy to my mind at rest.

I am so grateful for all that is before me
and the healing that is behind me.

Chapter Summary

Chapter 5 was rich with the pillars needed to enhance your healing practice and bring the thoughts and ideas from the previous chapters together. Chapters 1 and 2 provided vital information about your body and the need to connect to it consciously and subconsciously. By acknowledging the body sensations, you become aware of the communication your body is giving you. This vital information helped you learn how to be curious about sensations from your body communicating needed care. Learning mind patterns in chapter 4 and understanding how trauma shows up in chapter 3 laid the foundation for using what you have learned to incorporate the healing knowledge in your mind and body. This chapter provided real-life examples of healing experiences to illustrate Level 1: Body Sensations; Level 2: Mind Patterns; and Level 3: Reflective Tools and Positive Connection to Body, Mind, and Spirit.

Chapter 5 also provided information to deepen your understanding of how to enrich your connection with yourself. Muscle testing was discussed as another tool for checking in with your body and energy. Thinking patterns were explored with actual experiences to unpack unwanted trauma and models for removing deep belief systems. Energy medicine was introduced as a tool for connection and transformation of energy.

Chapter 5 introduced information on primary chakras to enhance the relationship between the body and mind. Tools like forgiveness, deep belief work, and younger selves enriched the healing landscape in this chapter. Various ways to connect to the self deeper were discussed throughout. Tools and resources for healing various feelings were layered in this chapter. This chapter also introduced new information to enhance and deepen your trauma healing through embodied activities and how to look for connections to body, mind, and spirit. This chapter gave many examples and resources for self-reflection and enhancing your healing journey. The tools of healing lead to the special connection of spirituality.

CHAPTER SIX
REFLECTIVE TOOLS
FOR RECONNECTION

This chapter will include information about how to incorporate new learning about trauma in the body and mind into regular care. It also provides self-reflection and care tools to continue paving new roads of healing, strengthening, and breaking free from past trauma to continue new avenues of wellness. Reflective writing prompts, questions, and planning templates are included throughout the chapter.

Trauma is the body's response to anything perceived as a harm. If the body thinks it is a threat, it responds. The body could react by fight, flight, fawn, or flock. Trauma responses can live in your body. At times, a response can occur without you realizing trauma was present. A threatening experience can leave the residue of trauma in your body. Bonnie Badenoch—author, therapist, and Founder of Nurturing the Heart with the Mind and Body—states in the book *Being a Brain-Wise Therapist*, "Hebb's axiom roughly says that what fires together, wires together, and now we might add, survives together. This concept means that all aspects of an experience tend to gather into a neural net that encodes a representation of that event. When one strand of that net is touched by current experience, there is some probability that the whole net will be activated. This is called remembering."[6] If an event has happened, a manifestation of the trauma could show up in your personality, habits, mood swings, choices in relationships, and general self-care.

Remember the trauma experience depicted in graphic 1 on page 40? Our bodies respond to trauma, and these descriptions are ways the body responds. No two people are alike, and our responses could include a number of these reactions or none that are listed. The most important task needed in the discovery of trauma is the ability to notice when our bodies are acting differently. A traumatic event could include many different events. The events are traumatic when our body senses it as a threat. The exploration of trauma and knowing the truth about it will help you see that an everyday event could trigger a response you did not expect. The uncertainty of the response is something to pay attention to in your body, with loved ones and people in your everyday life.

Fight, flight, freeze, flock, and fawn could be experienced in several ways. Fight represents a protection for safety. It can look like your body tightening, being impulsive or hyper, speaking sharply, grabbing something to protect yourself, or using physical force. Flight is the need to find safety by escaping. It could look like an increase in breathing, a tensing of the muscles, fainting, or running away. Freeze is the inability to think or move properly. If

---

6. Badenoch, *Being a Brain-Wise Therapist*.

you were to experience a freeze response, you could be paralyzed, feel heaviness in your limbs, have a feeling of doom, experience shallow breathing, or feel coldness in the body. Flock is finding safety with the others; it is to be in the safety of a group. This could look like going to places where there are groups of people to feel safe. Lastly, fawn is an attempt to portray that everything is going okay. Fawn could look like people-pleasing or going along with the group and never showing how you may feel. All these responses could show up in our day-to-day lives.

Do you remember the cycles of violence from graphic 2 on page 42? This graphic describes acting in experiences and acting out experiences. It is important for us to examine how we are responding to life in general. Are we responding with trauma responses? This graphic helps us see what we could not see before. If we find that our actions are aligned with acting in (harm to ourselves) or acting out (harm to others), it is time for reflection on what is causing us to behave that way. In addition to projecting outward harm and internal harm, it is important to not accumulate long-term effects from harm that has been unhealed. When we examine places in our lives, we also want to look for the telltale signs of trauma.

One of the truths about trauma is it masks itself as part of our personality when, with exploration, it is not. As you look at the graphic, do any of these responses subtly show in your daily life? Remain very curious in this chapter as you explore using the tools to discover and discard trauma responses and look to expand joy and light in your life. Every step toward healing is a wonderful exploration into positive energy. What could that look like in our world today? In this chapter, you will look to discover anything pulling your energy into negativity and transform it into energy that betters our lives.

Trauma Identification

Let's start by bringing awareness to what trauma may exist for you. What manifestations of trauma do you identify with from this list?

- Addiction
- Generational trauma
- Suicide
- Lawlessness
- Domestic violence
- Internalized oppression
- Difficulty working, hard work
- Numbing out; shutting down
- Unhealthy friendships/relationships
- Negative self-talk
- Feeling constantly behind
- Making something bigger than it needs to be; ignoring something that requires attention
- Being a victim/martyrdom
- Lack of empathy
- Egocentricity
- Exhaustion
- Cycles of panic
- Limited attention span
- Self-deprivation as a way to self-worth

Revisit this list as you continue your healing journey. Knowing how trauma shows up is good information to pay attention to in your healing journey.

Your Guide to Healing

You worked on getting to know your body and becoming aware of feelings in your body. You began creating a meditation practice at the beginning of this book. By now, you have developed and cultivated it. This meditative practice is one of the foundations you have built to assist you in discovering and discarding the harms of the past in your body, mind, and spirit. Information has been discussed on how to connect to the body. This information is a foundational beginning.

Your body has a journey of its own and it is important to establish a relationship with your body. You can ask your body questions and listen to its needs and desires. This journey is one of wonder. During this exploration you worked on getting to know your body and becoming aware of the connection between your body and mind. Using curiosity and tools provided in this book, you have had opportunities to observe your mind to understand feelings, sensations, and ideas that stand out. Using your agency of discovery and initiative, you now have the room to continue to wonder and heal areas that need care. The body is the control center to thoughts. Healing of the body and mind makes space for the spirit to be enlightened.

I found this newfound positive energy from healing to be electrifying. More and more I acted differently and was more patient, kind, and loving toward myself and others. My spiritual self continues to grow and lighten. This awareness may have been easier for some and perhaps difficult for others, yet learning to be one with your body, mind, and spirit is critical. Think back to the end of each chapter. Each chapter provided self-care tools, affirmations, meditations, and ritual practices. You may have found what speaks to you and can capture your preferences as best practices for your healing journey in this chapter.

The section that follows is to guide your healing. Now you get to take the time to reflect on all you have learned and capture your overall thoughts. First you will write goals for your healing. Write whatever comes to mind. This is a loving process and not a race. The next section will focus on the available tools and what feels most supportive for you. If there are tools that were not mentioned in this text but that you've discovered to be helpful, write them down as well. Step by step, you are building a pathway to healing.

We'll then have you look at body support: How do you best create foundational help for your body? Write down what works for your body. Support for the mind is next. You can see the building blocks on each idea and the pathway of your healing tools. In the mind support section, write about the basics of what you found to assist you in healing mind patterns. In the spiritual support section, capture the things that make your heart sing and cause your spirit to jump for joy. What are the things you find as supportive to your spirit? In the last section, summarize what you consider to be best practices or favorite tools for body, mind, and spirit. Here you will also list the resources that work best for you. You will see, by the end of this exercise, that you now have a depth of information to return to and utilize on your healing journey.

What Healing Feels Like

You will know you have healed and opened up more positive energy when you feel a flow of positive energy where the trauma response had previously held space. Each time I moved something, it was amazing how wonderful my energy rose. The same will happen for your journey. The result is mystic awakening to all that is. It is almost like someone took off a heavy blanket. The key is following the levels, making room for growth, and accepting the light of your spiritual self.

Capture any positive or joyful experiences you have had in your journal.

You will continue to hone more information about your body in the following section. This may seem repetitive, but remember: trauma is healed in layers. These various ways of traveling your healing journey will help you isolate and identify new layers of trauma and move deeper into the healing. The truth about trauma is it is hidden and requires a variety of healing methods to act as a blanket for exploration of the many healing pathways.

Goals

In your journal, utilize the following sentence starter to develop goals for healing. Develop three to five goals for healing body, mind, and spirit.

My goal for healing is to

_____.

Tools

In your journal, utilize the sentence starter to develop tools you prefer for your healing. Develop between three to five tools that you prefer. If you need to, check the Wellness Tool Kit on page 227 to refresh your memory on the tools we've covered throughout the book.

> *I will use the* _____
> *tool to address my healing.*

Body Supports

In your journal, utilize the sentence starter to develop optimum body supports for your healing. List between three to five body supports that work best.

> *My body support includes*
> _____.

Mind Supports

In your journal, utilize the sentence starter to capture tools that support your mind. List between three to five mind supports that work best.

> *My mind support includes*
> _____.

Spiritual Supports

In your journal, utilize the sentence starter to create the best spiritual support for your healing. List between three to five spiritual supports that work best.

My spiritual support includes
_____.

Best Personal Practices

In your journal, capture your favorite tool for body, mind, and spiritual connection. Describe what resources work best for your body, mind, and spirit.

In your journal, reflect on your personal understanding of topics covered in previous chapters. This reflection will assist you in gathering your thoughts and understanding of the information you have learned.

Journal Reflection: Reconnection

Use the prompts below to capture your reflections about the previous section in your journal. These guiding prompts are provided to assist you in this reflection process.

- Describe what you understand about your body, mind, and spirit.
- Capture what you have learned from versions of younger selves.
- Report what you learned about your belief systems.
- Describe learning about your energy centers or chakras.
- Describe what you learned about forgiveness.
- Overall reflect on the learning and healing from the previous chapters.
- Describe what other parts of your healing you are curious to know.

- Describe your learning about manifestations of trauma in your life.

- What kind of trauma is showing up most in your life? (Refer to chapter 3 to recall the types of trauma.)

- What have you learned about sources of trauma in your life?

- Use the information you have gathered about your body. In your journal, list body sensations you are curious to heal.

Using the Healing Roadmap Framework

Now, it is time for the healing aspects of how you will break free from the manifestations of trauma in your life. After identifying where in your body and personality trauma has shown up, it is essential to gather more information about the trauma through your mind patterns and thinking. Your thinking promotes healing, which is why it is necessary to interrupt negative thinking. Meditation and self-care help can be used to interrupt thinking that will not assist your healing. Many tools have been discussed in these pages, and each will work differently for each individual.

The Healing Roadmap Framework is a tool provided to assist you with using the three levels that lead to healing. Each section is designed to provide a structure to assist you. Here's an example of what it looks like to walk through the framework—we'll dive in deeper in future sections as well:

> Level 1: What incident has occurred that you want to examine more deeply?
> *For example: I am uncomfortable and frightened when I hear people screaming.*

Write your wondering in your journal.

> Level 2: What tool would you like to use to find out more about this feeling?
> *For example: I plan to use meditation and emotional tapping to calm my body and mind. Then I will use the Thinking Map to dig deeper into the feelings.*

List in your journal what tools you are going to use.

> Level 3: Do you need to do additional healing for your chakras or energy centers, meridians, younger selves, forgiveness, or deep belief systems?
> *The Breaking Free and Reconnection tools of Level 3 are intended to help you break free from trauma. Nothing happens overnight, but each time I have used any of these tools, I have been released from the trauma that held me one step at a time. If your healing takes time, do not feel overwhelmed or that you are not on the right track. That is not true.*

Using Tools to Interrupt Trauma and Break Free

Interrupting trauma and breaking free involves staying aware of your body's signals and using healing tools and methods to work through that trauma.

For example, if you find that one or more of your chakras are blocked, explore healing meditations for them. The directions for the healing meditation for chakras are in chapter 5.

To clear your meridians, which are the highway of your energy, you can use the emotional tapping resource in chapter 3.

Use your new skill of muscle testing to gauge your energy of the following emotions: enlightenment, peace, joy, love, reason, acceptance, willingness, neutrality, courage, pride, anger, desire, fear, grief, apathy, guilt, and shame.

When something comes up that feels much like your seven-year-old self, you can use the tools of younger versions of selves to address healing. Review the example on page 143.

If you choose forgiveness as a tool, you can follow the information on page 162. If you find yourself needing to remove old belief patterns, you can follow the directions on page 113.

Let's look closer at tools you can use to support your healing under the three categories: body connection, mind patterns, and spiritual healing.

Body Connection Tools

Review the following tools and list in your journal which you have used to care for your body and what your experience was.

- ACES quiz
- Guided meditation
- Box breathing
- Pursed lip breathing
- 4-7-8 breathing
- Movement
- Finger holds
- Emotional tapping
- Visualization
- Music
- Alternate nostril breathing
- Table 1: Results of Trauma
- Exercise
- Nature
- Food choices
- Embodied art
- Embodied voice art
- Energy medicine
- Breathwork

Mind Pattern Tools

Review the list of mind pattern tools in Table 6, and use the following prompts to write your thoughts in your journal:

- List mind patterns you are curious to heal.
- What tools have you used to interrupt mind patterns?
- What tools did you use to break free?

- Thinking Map
- Box breathing
- Pursed lip breathing
- 4-7-8 breathing
- Chakras
- Meridians
- Younger selves
- Finger holds
- Emotional tapping
- Visualization
- Music
- Guided meditation
- Exercise
- Nature
- Embodied art
- Embodied voice art
- Forgiveness
- Energy medicine
- Breathwork

Spiritual Tools

Use the prompts below to capture your reflections about the list of spiritual tools in Table 7 in your journal.

- What spiritual tools have you learned to use in your healing journey?
- Have you healed and felt the expansion of your spiritual life?
- What is missing from your spiritual development?

- Grounding
- Regular meditation
- High-vibrational foods: white meat, vegetables, pineapples, papayas, lemons, and oranges

- Increase water intake
- Work with deep belief system
- Reduction of negative behavior, thoughts, and actions

Healing Roadmap Framework

The Healing Roadmap Framework below is for you to utilize when you need to go through the level system with a trauma response. You will make this framework your own. Below you will see the structure of the healing process for you to use moving forward.

> Level 1
> *What incident has occurred that you want to examine more deeply?*

> Level 2
> *What tool would you like to use to find out more about this feeling?*

> Level 3
> *Do you need to do additional healing for your chakras or energy centers, meridians, younger selves, forgiveness, or deep belief systems?*

Use this list when you are curious about what is going on in your body. This list can serve as a starting place as you move through the healing levels.

- What healing did you observe?
- How did you break free from the trauma?
- How does your body feel?
- How does your mind feel?
- How does your spirit feel?
- What worked well for you?
- Did you use something you have not used before?
- What is next on your healing journey?

Self-Care Tools: Reconnection

Explore these self-care tools as you continue to build on and deepen your reconnection practice.

Affirmations

Consider the following affirmations for your healing.

Level 1

I am connected to my body.

I want to heal my body, mind, and spirit.

Write an affirmation in your journal.

Level 2

My thoughts are positive.

My thoughts are loving, kind, and peaceful.

Write an affirmation in your journal.

Level 3

I am worthy.

I love my body, mind, and spirit.

I am free of harm.

I am courageously healing.

Write an affirmation in your journal.

Meditation

Start this meditation with the White Light Prayer.

> *In the name of Source (universe, God, I am, etc.), I ask for the highest white light and vibration on the right of me and the left of me, all around me and through me, over my head and under my feet in all spaces known and unknown.*
>
> *Let there be no interference right here, right now, and so it is in the name of Source.*
>
> *Find a comfortable place and gently close your eyes.*
>
> *Breathe in through your nose and out slowly through your mouth, purse your lips, and let the air move slowly as you exhale from your mouth.*
>
> *Breathe in through your nose and out slowly through your mouth, purse your lips, and let the air move slowly as you exhale from your mouth.*
>
> *Breathe in through your nose and out slowly through your mouth, purse your lips, and let the air move slowly as you exhale from your mouth.*

> *With your eyes closed, reach your senses out and*
> *pay attention to any sensations that are not the ones*
> *you usually feel. Be curious.*
> *When you are ready, slowly come out of meditation.*

Rituals

Continue building on the loving and self-caring rituals you've established.

Morning

Upon waking, take a deep breath and set your intention about the day before you get up.

> *I am capable and calm.*
>
> *I am capable and calm.*
>
> *I am capable and calm.*

Grounding

When you put your feet on the ground, take another deep breath. Focus pulling energy from the crown of your head, down your body, and out the soles of your feet to the floor, down into the earth. Take another deep breath and pull new fresh energy from the earth up through your feet, up your body, up to the crown of your head. Take your time to feel the power of the energy rise up your body.

Noon

Pause at noon and review your affirmation for the day.

I am capable and calm.

I am capable and calm.

I am capable and calm.

If you can make space, take time for a small meditation or some kind of peaceful movement.

Evening

*In gratitude and loving-
kindness I bring this day to a close.*

May I slumber in peace and nourishment.

*In my rest, bring the light of all light upon me in
the same way the universe has granted me peace.*

Chapter Summary

This chapter modeled how to incorporate the learnings from previous chapters. The chapter reviewed what trauma was and how it shows up in your body. Trauma experiences manifest in various ways, listed in this chapter to assist you. The chapter sets you up to reflect on your preferred tools on your healing journey. The Healing Roadmap Framework is provided to lead you toward examining your harms using the three levels of healing. The Breaking Free section guides you through the tools to use in your healing journey. It is a pathway to help you work on healing by working through the levels step-by-step. The framework guides you through reflection on the levels, starting with body sensations, then moving through mind patterns, and incorporating spiritual tools for enhancement. The Healing Roadmap Framework leads you through the healing process from beginning to end. This chapter provides the path forward to assist you on your healing journey.

CHAPTER SEVEN
HEALING FROM TRAUMA

This chapter will highlight my experiences of how I healed trauma in my family system, as well as in the areas of abuse, addiction, race and gender discrimination, and sexual identity.

Much can be written about life struggles from many different avenues. In this chapter, I will chronicle my healing and how I found peace and freedom using the tools I have shared with you in this book. Everything in this book has come from my personal experiences healing trauma in my life. As previously mentioned, I did not set out to know about trauma or heal from it. The most magical part about my healing journey is that the universe led me to each healer and modality, and that is what I am sharing with you. There is hope for change—I have seen it and so can you.

Healing within Family Systems

Family systems bring many feelings, attitudes, and experiences of joy and sorrow. This area was the hardest for me to heal and examine. I felt that if I looked at my family's actions that harmed me, I was betraying the family system. In my context, family systems describe the relationships of the people who raised me or whom I spent considerable time with during my formative years and upbringing. My search for healing came at a time when I had to examine these systems, as my experiences had colored my personality and interfered with my healthy relationship building with others. It does not mean I did not love my family because I discussed my experiences and healed them for myself. I think that point is critical. You are not betraying your family if you work on healing yourself. Keep that in mind because traumatic experiences can shut down change, even if it is for the best. In the following section, I will give concrete examples of what I healed concerning my family system and how I used the tools outlined in this book. In my family, I experienced emotional, physical, and sexual abuse.

Mind Patterns/Deep Belief System

Harm in formative years can damage energy centers and sense of self. Through the experiences of my upbringing, I believed something was wrong with me and that I was flawed. I learned this through the work of Cheri Huber, Zen Monk student, teacher, and writer. Why did I need to know this before I went into healing? My healing needed to be on a foundation of love and care. When I started, I did not have that love and care for myself. Subconsciously, I believed there was something wrong with me. Why else would people who were supposed to be there to care for me have treated me that way? Those thoughts were subconscious. Learning about Cheri Huber's work taught me that I needed to get right with myself so I could heal. I had to take myself off the hook. If I did not, the healing work would be shallow and continue to linger. Before I could heal anything, I had to realize and unlearn what I had been socialized to:

- Think there was something wrong with me
- Examine my flaws continuously
- Judge my flaws, not heal them
- Hate me for being who I am
- Punish myself so I can change

Instead, what I needed to do is the following:

- To love myself for the good in me
- To appreciate myself for who I am
- To trust myself
- To have confidence in my abilities
- To look to my heart, higher self, and spirituality for guidance

I had to admit that I cycled in self-hatred and needed to move into awareness of the ego-critic mind to diminish it and operate from a loving paradigm. What I am proposing is big. These ideas are the foundation of my success. Not only did I do the healing, I did it from this standpoint. Because I started here, I could work at a much deeper level than if I had not taken time to make this critical shift of energy. Willingness is the key to creating the bedrock for healing. After establishing self-love as a foundation, I could begin to heal from trauma.

Here are examples of deep belief systems that I needed to transform. These beliefs were based on my thinking patterns and needed to be replaced with positive beliefs for healing.

~~I don't know how to heal my relationships.~~
I can learn how to heal my relationships.

~~I can't learn to understand my family.~~
I can learn to understand my family.

~~People I love abandon me.~~
People I love love me and support me.

~~I am not loved.~~
I am deeply loved.

~~People disappoint me.~~
People delight and surprise me.

~~I can't count on others.~~
I can count on some others.

~~It's difficult to consciously create my reality.~~
It is easy to consciously create my reality.

How did I acquire these beliefs? Some I found through working with supportive materials like Boni Lonnsbury's *Map of Abundance*. Other beliefs I found in exploration through journaling, energy medicine, bodywork, coaching, and intuition. Through these deep explorations, I found beliefs that did not align with who I was and wanted to become.

Healing Sexual and Physical Abuse

One of the primary places to examine healing is starting with the body. As a survivor of sexual abuse, part of me learned to ignore my body and the sensations around my body. The exploration of body sensations began for me through guided meditation and body awareness. I started to accept that I was uncomfortable with people standing very close, in my peripheral vision, or touching certain body parts. I thought these were preferences. These were my preferences based on past harms. Beginning with massages/bodywork, I began to have a relationship with my body, which helped me support the relationship with my thinking and mind in healing.

A cousin sexually abused me when I was four years old. The lingering trauma response showed up in several ways in my life. Sadly, I did not receive any counseling or comfort about what had happened. A close family member punished me for being abused. I know it is harsh to read and hard to accept, but that is what happened. In turn, my body adapted some foundational systems in processing my sexual identity and relationship with my body. The introduction of sexuality and sexual feelings at a young age is not only abusive, it also colors the natural relationship with sex, identity, gender, and the body as a whole.

The root chakra is the first energy center and the foundation. My root chakra was damaged from this early encounter. In turn, my family did not know how to support me. I felt the family blamed me for the abuse. I was scrutinized for where I went, what I was doing, what I looked like, how much weight I carried, and what clothes I chose to wear. All these interactions, on top of the abuse, colored how I reacted to the world and those around me.

Let's look at aspects of healing. Healing did not happen from one event, like the harm did; it occurred over many intersections with other healing. The first part of healing is admitting there was a problem.

So, the first part of my healing came from journaling about what happened factually. The journaling gave me information about what occurred that I would use for the healing aspects, without coloring it with opinions or other feelings. I am not going to lie; it was hard to do. I had support, and I recommend you get support for diving into something as painful and debilitating as childhood sexual abuse. What support looked like for me was that I had several friends doing the same work, so I had a support group. I had a mentor whom I talked to regularly about healing, and I sought a specialist in the mental health field. So, I was not alone.

The next step for me was to clear the space in my body where I believed that I had caused this abuse. It was not anything I had said to myself, but it was an unspoken energy that accompanies abuse. I needed to change my thinking and let go of the false narrative of responsibility. Letting go of responsibility was challenging to accomplish. One place I found deep healing was healing the chakras colored by the abuse.

Healing the Chakras

I was unfamiliar with chakras before I started doing the work to heal. I was willing to try anything and found profound healing, and energy returned to my body after chakra healing. I followed a chakra meditation that took me to an unhealed place. I did not know where I would end up. I was at the scene of my abuse. I saw what happened to me as a child. It was hard to watch. The meditation suggested I focus on the person committing the harm and consider what brought them to this situation. Honestly, I did not want to focus on my cousin who harmed me, but I did it. When I was ready, I released both souls, myself and my cousin, to the light. For me, this meditation worked well. The meditation helped me complete the healing work I had focused on for many years in many ways. Do not be discouraged if you find yourself healing something in different ways more than once. This chakra healing left me with a new rush of positive energy afterward.

I used chakra healing on physical abuse that continued to stay with me in adulthood. A parent harmed me through corporal punishment for something I did not do. The harm lingered on my throat chakra. I was surprised to find this constriction in my throat chakra. I used meditation to clear and heal my chakras and found that my throat chakra was constricted. Through journaling and meditation, I was taken back to the experience when I was young and punished severely. The intersectionality of abuse is complex. I suffered physical harm that affected my ability to advocate for myself as an adult. These healings are not a one-and-done. The healing cycle continues to refine the body, mind, and spirit.

Every person is different, and abuse has a myriad of complexities. My message is to begin with self-love, old beliefs, and body connection and use what is calling to you for healing. Clearing my energy centers brought love and light into my body.

What did I learn about my family system? I knew that more than likely, physical and sexual abuse was a generational trauma in our family system. It was not discussed or talked about openly or privately. I did not try to change minds and hearts to address the harm I healed myself. I sought to examine why I was carrying so much trauma in general from this lifetime and past trauma from previous lifetimes. I knew my family origin was from Africa, and my people lived through slavery. I experienced lingering historical, cultural, and generational trauma. This journey has brought the ripple effect of healing to my immediate family. When I was ready, I got additional healing to each damaged relationship through forgiveness. This forgiveness tool brought immense freedom and light to my spirit.

Forgiveness Steps
- Be completely ready to let go
- Start with a prayer of light and truth
- Write what the person has done
- Forgive them for their actions
- Ask for forgiveness for my ill feelings

Healing Addictions

I would not have named myself as a person who would fall to addictions. When I was eighteen years old, I struggled with living, and I made a conscious decision to numb out by using alcohol and drugs. I did not want to be present in my life. Addiction was a constant battle of lack of care with an unkind mental obsession. Once I was free of addiction, a path of destruction was left in the aftermath. Addictions are a form of self-hatred and neglect. At the time of abuse, I did not think so, but looking in the rearview mirror, it is evident that I was responding to trauma by trying to drown myself in altered states. The core of my addictive behavior was grounded in the self-hatred of who I was and my flaws. I could not accept who I was, and the way I felt better about it was something that made me feel worse.

What broke this horrible spell? It was a spiritual experience. A powerful spiritual experience took place in which I felt like I suddenly woke up. My life was spared to complete the work I am doing now, shining light on parts of living that need light—taking feelings like shame, despair, and unworthiness out of the shadows and wrapping them in healing light.

To break free from addiction, you must free your mind. You control your mind; your mind does not control you. There are many healing ways to do so, but there is something special for you, and the universe knows what it is. I am not here to tell you what your path is, but if you want a path with all your heart and soul, whether you believe it or not, the universe is there for you; there is hope and it can emerge. That may seem noncommittal, but it is not. You can reverse self-hatred. Before I could heal anything, I had to realize and unlearn. I had been socialized to:

- Think there was something wrong with me
- Examine my imperfections continuously
- Judge my imperfections, not heal them
- Hate myself for being who I am
- Punish myself so I can change, which is addiction

What I needed to do for healing was the following:

- To love myself for the good in me
- To appreciate myself for who I am; my core good
- To trust myself

- To have confidence in my abilities; I can do it!
- To look to my heart, higher self, and spirituality for guidance

I had to admit that I cycled in self-hatred and needed to move into awareness of the ego-critic mind to diminish it and operate from a loving paradigm. This is what is needed to break free, and I know from experience that it is a struggle to be back in charge of your body, mind, and soul. Support is helpful. Aloneness is fatal. Once you can control your mind, you have a chance to be free.

It took me a while for my spirit and body to merge back together after addiction. I failed at stopping a few times. It was the loneliness and lack of support that pulled me back into addiction. I could control my ego-critic mind and self-hatred with support and patience. It took time and a lot of self-love, and everyone's journey is different. Self-love is foundational, as shown by taking action and belief work, as indicated by control and retraining your mind.

Addictions are full of the harms that occur within the addiction lifestyle. The foundational work of self-love through action and belief work to control your mind are massive undertakings. The number of harms that arise for others and yourself is a haunting existence while working on the latter. I experienced many harms in addiction, and I also harmed those I love and care about greatly. The foundation of moving forward requires waiting in the tunnel to feel the healing that is coming. I know I wanted the healing, resolution, and forgiveness to be given right away. The harm occurred over time, and healing happens over time. To stop addiction, build a good foundation of love through actions and control the negative warring mind. Sorry, it's not an answer you can buy at the store. It is an answer that will set a foundation for health.

Look for resources for addictions in the back of the book.

Healing Racial Trauma

Experiences of racial trauma catapulted my healing journey. In the study of my life experiences as a Black woman working in organizations, I found that I experienced racial trauma four times more than healing. In that research, I discovered healing from racial trauma. I found a way up and out of suffering by seeking peace from racial harm. This book is on that healing. I believed I could heal racial trauma by focusing on what happened and working through it. That was not wholly true. I needed to heal my past trauma first so I could clearly understand and identify my racial trauma. My trauma healing, in general, allowed me to heal from the foundation of racial trauma in my life and address new issues with ease and comfort. I had to examine the foundations of who I was and heal the trauma that continued to live in my body; when I did that, I could begin healing generational and historical trauma from the past and the present.

What is racial trauma? Racial trauma is similar to PTSD. It is a trauma based on individual and collective experiences of race-based stress. In the article "Racial Trauma: Theory, Research, and Healing" by Lillian Comas-Díaz, Gordon Nagayama Hall, and Helen A. Neville, race-based stress experiences may include threats of "harm and injury, humiliating and shaming events, and witnessing racial discrimination toward other People of Color and Indigenous individuals (POCI) ongoing individual and collective injuries due to exposure and reexposure to race-based stress."[7] Racial trauma involves instances where the individual may feel the experiences of harm but cannot articulate a tangible reason for the discomfort. The feeling of oppression is a real one, and yet it is explicit in discussions about racial harm. Often, the focus is on what the person did to you. The idea that a feeling or body sensation is the foundation of stress is ignored; therefore, the person discriminated against suffers in silence because they do not have any tangible proof. This quiet suffering becomes problematic as the individual begins to take action to protect themselves, and much like a steam kettle, the small bits and pieces of fighting back become the evidence that the person harmed is the problem.

This web is universal for all those experiencing harm in any way through the negative neurotoxins of others. Racial trauma can be seen and not seen, and the critical fact is the person who is experiencing the harm must learn how to regulate their healing. We often witness a person's anger and attempts to fight back. In those scenarios, we do not see the thousand paper cuts of harm that push an individual out of their window of tolerance or calm state of being.

Racial harm can be overt or covert. Overt racial harm includes incidents that are meant as discrimination. Covert racial harm is more subtle and passive; it includes practices of oppression in society that have not been unlearned or exposed as oppressive. Covert racial harm is often categorized as a misunderstanding or presented as "I did not mean to" rationalization.

I experienced race-based stress in my occupation that manifested into health problems. This manifestation of trauma got my

7. Comas-Díaz, Hall, and Neville, "Racial Trauma," 1.

attention, and I was dumbfounded that I was unable to self-rescue from a job that was killing me or be able to identify the harm. I ignored body sensations, and my mind patterns continued interrupting my healing. I think many people experience this kind of trauma—both people of color and those who are advocates for equity, diversity, and inclusion. What none of us planned for was the trauma we experience in our attempts to fulfill the intention of inclusion in our world. For people of color, the invisibilization of race-based stress coupled with cultural, historical, and generational trauma is a problem and a foundation of cycles of harm. Advocates of equality, non–people of color, face a similar fate; their historical and generational trauma transfers the energy of trauma from their experiences and the experiences of their ancestry. When advocates continue to push systems to be inclusive, they, too, experience harmful oppressive practices. What does this mean? It means that we all have healing to do in this area and that our common welfare is what matters. We are all part of the world, meaning racial healing is for everyone.

There is a specific focus for people of color. You have some work to do to heal those macro- and microaggressions you experience walking down the street, at work, and in the community. Processing racial harm can mirror anger, hatred, self-hatred, and the perpetuation of dominance and power, which is not helpful. Trying harder, putting yourself in more harm to fight the system, stuffing, or ignoring your feelings is not beneficial for processing racial harm. What is useful is healing past harms. To examine racial trauma, you must heal the trauma that is at the foundation of your experiences and being; when you do that, you can begin to heal the racialized trauma in a way that will bring peace and light into your life. This book is a perfect place to start. You will find that you will have space in your body, mind, and soul to use self-love and reflection to heal after healing the past first.

Racial trauma is trauma, and it is centered in the body. For example, someone at work may say something to you, and suddenly, you have this feeling in your body. It doesn't feel right. Next, you dismiss it, or the thoughts cycle in and out of your mind. You may mention it to a friend who identifies with your culture or ethnicity. Your friend, in turn, will minimize your experience or have big feelings about it. In turn, you are left with unresolved energy of harm.

Remember body sensations? This is it. You may dismiss this sensation because you cannot substantiate what it is. Let's stop right there. This part of trauma happens for all kinds of traumas. Something is said or done, the body has a sensation, and the mind dismisses it. What occurs over time is the body continues to stack up these harms until they manifest into something else like high blood pressure, mood swings, or depression. Remember mind patterns; this is it too. Your mind, ego, and critical mind will not allow you to examine the harm. This is the same as the other harms I have reviewed in this chapter. The belief pattern must be interrupted so that healing can take place. I have talked to countless people who dismiss their experiences of harm over and over and over again.

What Racial Trauma Looks Like

Racial trauma can manifest in many different forms; below are some of the most pervasive:

- Ignoring a person of color when they greet you or talk to you
- Walking into a person of color on a shared walkway or sidewalk like they don't exist
- Not waiting on a person of color when they are next in line
- Assuming a person's nationality or ethnicity
- Calling someone by slang terms, ignoring their name and position

Healing is available for all of us. First, admit there is a problem. Listen to your body sensations. Name the harm. What kind of harm is it? Then, get on the journey of healing in general and then more specifically. I am not suggesting remaining in harmful situations. I recommend using the outline in this book to begin the healing process. Always find safety when you need it.

Race relations remain unhealed in the United States. I have also found similar relationships to be unhealed in other parts of the world. When one group has harmed another, the energy of healing typically does not manifest without effort. The world needs to change this paradigm to one of healing.

For those on the journey of healing racialized trauma, I have created a framework for healing based on what has been shared in this book. To engage fully, remove past harms, and realize and unlearn. We all have been socialized to doubt ourselves. We have learned this by how we have been treated in the world. If your mind is pushing back, ask yourself why. This is not an attack on your family systems or the community you grew up in. We all have had a similar experience or we would not be reading this book. Society has taught us that:

- There is something wrong with you
- You must look at your imperfections all the time
- You must judge your imperfections, not heal them
- You must hate yourself for who you are and not being perfect
- You must punish yourself so you can change, not change your actions or belief systems

What you needed to do for healing is the following:

- To love yourself for the good in you
- To appreciate yourself for who you are; at your core, you are good
- To trust yourself
- To have confidence in your abilities; you can do anything!
- To look to your heart, higher self, and spirituality for guidance

When you interrupt your mind patterns and connect to your body for help, the road opens for new adventures. Try it. We all need this world as a place to center community wellness in racial healing.

Healing Gender Trauma

The world has changed quite a bit since I was born in 1965. I want to touch on gender because it is an ever-present topic in trauma and one that is generally ignored. We have seen in recent years how women have come forward to discuss the trauma of being mistreated. These public vulnerabilities are often met with traumatizing commentary and more harm. I want to name gender trauma that is alive and present in many ways in our society. We see this microcosm of mistreatment with women, men, sexual identity, and sexual fluidity. This topic sheds light on those who continue to suffer traumatic abuse in the oppressive structures we work and live in. The tools in this book are intended to bring healing to those who suffer.

You are not alone, and this book's level system works for all traumas. The steps are the same for the family system trauma as they are for gender and sexual identity trauma. First, you must admit you are experiencing trauma. Then, you need to be willing to unlearn what you think about yourself and relearn that you are good, trusting, and appreciative of yourself by looking to your heart for guidance. To find your heart, you cannot be spinning on the cycles of violence, as shown in the image on page 42.

This graphic represents the ongoing cycling of trauma from self-hatred inside to self-hatred outside of yourself. These trauma responses become exasperated over time. Our job is to care for ourselves and break away from trauma responses by acknowledging harm when it occurs.

In our everyday lives, we hear comments that center on gender in one way or another:

- Are you strong enough to pull that off? It's a man's work.
- I do not know anything about making coffee; I am a man.
- Hi honey, or hi sweetie, or let me get that, darling.
- We can't hire her; she looks like a man.
- I don't get pronouns; I am not using them.

If you are experiencing gendered trauma, please do not ignore it. Use this book's meditations, self-care tools, and suggestions to process the trauma and walk toward healing.

Healing Trauma Based on Sexual Identity

Sexual identity is personal and yet has been a focus of politics and policies in organizations and governments. So many constraints bound the human right to be who you are. It is traumatizing and challenging to find community and healing. In today's age, this topic continues to be in the public eye. We are hurting when it comes to treating people with dignity. If you have been mistreated, this section will remind you that you matter. Your health and well-being are important. Isolation and aloneness are the worst combination for trauma.

The first step mentioned previously is to admit you have experienced trauma or harm. Trauma is the worst thing to push away because it does not go away. It changes into something else. The truth about trauma is it will show up in another form. Our bodies try to protect us, which is why when a trauma occurs, it gets pushed away. The problem is that well-meaning people lose jobs, relationships, or friendships from unhealed trauma. People have been physically harmed in the cycles of trauma. The important thing about each person's experience is that we must tell our minds that goodness and wellness are not a pie. As in, if you have wellness, I can't have any. We all get to be well and live in peace if we choose. If you have experienced trauma based on your identity, you deserve to heal and be at peace.

When I met my wife and we got engaged, I told people in the office where I worked. I was so excited about my news. "I did not know she was gay!" the assistant principal of the school exclaimed in the office without thinking about how it sounded or how I might feel about her statement. A friend came and told me and suggested no longer sharing news about me with the assistant principal as she was not supportive. That was a harm.

Acknowledgment of harm brings the power of healing. I have outlined many tools in this writing. My prayer is that many work for you and your life. The most important thing I could ask is that you realize trauma is real and invisible. Do not ignore it; hug it and bring it close so you can get to know it, heal it, and transform it.

In these last few sections, I have discussed places where trauma can show up. This is not at all inclusive. The information here is a place you can revisit as you refine your practice of trauma healing through acknowledgment, getting to know your body, controlling your mind, and allowing your spirit to soar.

Healing through Community Well-Being

I have mentioned support throughout the book. What exactly does a supportive community look like? In healing, it is important to have a place to talk about whatever you need. Communities of well-being include places where attunement is part of the group's culture. I see few of these communities among us. We deserve a welcoming place to go and experience attunement and care. These community well-being locations can be in every town near or far. What is preventing us from beginning these kinds of engagements? In this work, think about others who are doing the same personal care. Create communities where attunement is a way of life with people who are aligned with healing and can be available to each other. A revolution of care is a good start.

Creating Support Systems for Healing

Create a system that supports your healing. That system can look like whatever you need for support. Examine the wellness tools at the end of each chapter. A system of support can include all those who are there for you in your hours of need, friends who are on the same journey, or medical professionals or mental health professionals who know about you and your journey. The most important thing here is that you have a thought-out support system as you examine trauma experiences. You are not going at it alone.

Who are the people who are supporting you in your journey?

Chapter Summary

This last chapter discusses what healing can look like in our lives. We live in a community with others, and our day-to-day experiences inevitably involve them. This chapter offers examples of challenges and healing experiences in family systems, sexual and physical harm, addictions, gender, and sexual identity. These complex topics are shared using real-life experiences to model healing. Sharing real-life experiences engages each topic from a place of hope for healing. Learning to heal is an up-and-down journey and requires a loving and welcoming community of supportive people. This chapter ends with encouragement and guidance to create your own system for healing support that will pave the way for consistent growth and wellness.

FINAL THOUGHTS

I don't have all the answers to healing, but what I do have is what has worked for me, which I've shared with you in this book. Throughout my journey, I've learned that when we bring healing to any situation, we bring love, and when we bring love, we bring light, and when we bring light, we bring the spirit of the universe. I have learned that my body is the portal to my soul and mind. When I can communicate with my body, I have insight into what has harmed me, what needs healing, and what is healed. When I take those actions over time, I am free, and my spirit is light. A light spirit is full of joy, bliss, and oneness with all there is. This is the place I like to reside—in oneness with all there is, with the ability to connect with my soul, walk hand in hand with the universe, and connect to my support on this plane and other planes to know the gift of healing. You don't have to walk the way I have walked, but do join me on this healing journey of freedom from harm and submission into the light.

I've also learned that trauma healing takes time, and reading this book is a massive step toward freedom in your journey. During your work through this book, you have become familiar with my healing and knowledge. But more importantly, as you read through the pages, you have learned about yourself. Your healing journey has started. It is a huge step. To peel back the layers of trauma and find true healing will take time. At times, it will not feel easy. Yet, hope and serenity lie in your ability to continue loving yourself through actions that help remove trauma residue from your life. Please continue to revisit this book and review the trauma healing information, highlighting your most treasured tools.

Reflecting on our journey together, we've learned that trauma happens in the body. It's not just an emotional response but the body's reaction to protection. This knowledge is crucial in processing our experiences in our bodies. The imprint of our experiences is the undercurrent of our thinking, feelings, and actions. But the joy of healing trauma is that we can remove trauma memories and pave new pathways. This joy will motivate you to continue your healing journey, filled with hope and optimism.

Doing the important work to learn to understand the body is the principle reason behind the vast collection of the healing resources provided in this book. At the beginning of the book, you learn to understand the body, trauma sources, and examples of how trauma can appear in everyday life. Then, you were ready to start the trauma healing journey by using this information to bring awareness to where your body, mind, and spirit may need healing. Each part of this book is a stepping stone toward new learning and growth as you read through the pages and participate in journal writings and reflections connecting you to your knowledge. As you built on new ideas, you took steps toward your growth through meditations, affirmations, and reflection rituals.

Healing the body and mind makes space for the spirit to be free. The later parts of the book focus on cultivating all three elements of body, mind, and soul for peaceful living. Activities are suggested to amplify these elements in one's life to remain connected to one's true self. Hopefully by this point, you have discovered your favorite self-care tools and healing activities as you explored what worked for you.

As we find what healing tools work for us and begin our healing journey, we must acknowledge the challenges of life living in and around us. We live in a world with people and processes that have jagged edges, and sometimes these edges hurt. Using these tools, we can care for ourselves no matter the circumstances. We can revisit the tools and how we feel, notice our bodies, and stop to breathe.

Recognizing trauma in the body, paying attention to the mind, and participating in self-care tools continue to build the framework for healing.

As you continue to walk your healing journey, I encourage you to keep this book close by and continue experimenting and exploring the tools and activities to deepen your self-love and overall healing. I also encourage you to keep the Healing Roadmap Framework close by. Take a snapshot and save it on your phone, jot down the steps onto a sticky note and post it on your refrigerator, or even make a copy of that page to use as your guide when working through triggers going forward.

Healing is not a one-time action but a cycle of self-love for improvement. Self-love is a revolutionary act that takes commitment and courage. And healing takes practice. It takes patience. It takes perseverance.

This healing is not to be done alone. We need each other. I am with you in this journey and will continue to provide resources for community and healing to accompany this book.

Stay in touch and know that I am with you on these pages and in healing. Let the love of our healing bring us closer to the love and light of peace we deserve.

ACKNOWLEDGMENTS

Completing a work of love takes an entire village. I want to acknowledge my wife and cheerleader, Amy Cox, who has celebrated all of my projects, especially this one.

None of this work would have come to life without the guidance and wisdom of Anthony J. W. Benson. He is a guiding light of inspiration.

I am grateful to Llewellyn decision-makers for taking on this project and envisioning it with us. Writing requires the eyes and ears of a hands-on editor. Danielle Anderson, thank you for being by my side. Throughout my journey on a healing path, I had the honor of working with some powerful women who carry love and light in this world. Cyndi Dale has impacted my life significantly through her books, writings, and wisdom. It is the most incredible honor for her to write the foreword of this book.

For over twenty-four years, Pat Yeo has been a guiding force in my life, helping shape me into the woman I am today. Reverend

AdaRA L. Walton has been another indispensable guide and close spiritual mentor who has helped me keep my feet on the ground. I want to acknowledge my ancestors, my strong line of spiritual women, and my parents for making space for my creativity.

Last, I thank the universe for guiding me and putting such loving people in my path so that I could manifest this work for anyone in need.

WORKS REFERENCED

Andrews, Ted. *How to Meet and Work with Spirit Guides.* Llewellyn Publications, 2006.

Badenoch, Bonnie. *Being a Brain-Wise Therapist: A Practical Guide to Interpersonal Neurobiology.* W. W. Norton & Company, 2008.

Brave Heart, M. Y., and L. M. DeBruyn. "The American Indian Holocaust: Healing Historical Unresolved Grief." *American Indian and Alaska Native Mental Health Research: Journal of the National Center* 8, no. 2: 56–78.

Burk, Connie, and Laura van Dernoot Lipsky. *Trauma Stewardship: An Everyday Guide to Caring for Self While Caring for Others.* Berrett-Koehler Publishers, 2009.

Collins, Lisa Y. "Healing Racial Trauma from Public School Systems." *Journal of Research Initiatives* 8 (2023).

Conscious Freedom Coaching. http://consciousfreedom coaching.com/.

Comas-Díaz, L., G. N. Hall, and H. A. Neville. "Racial Trauma: Theory, Research, and Healing: Introduction to the Special Issue." *American Psychologist* 74, no. 1 (2019): 1.

"Counselling for Relationships & Attachment: What Is Attachment?" https://www.enduringmind.co.uk/counselling-for-relationships-and-attachment/.

Dale, Cyndi. *Energy Healing for Trauma, Stress & Chronic Illness: Uncover & Transform the Subtle Energies That Are Causing Your Greatest Hardships.* Llewellyn Publications, 2020.

Dale, Cyndi. *Healing Through the Chakras.* Sounds True, 2011.

Dale, Cyndi. *New Chakra Healing: Activate Your 32 Energy Centers.* Llewellyn Publications, 1996.

Degruy, Joy. *Post Traumatic Slave Syndrome: America's Legacy of Enduring Injury and Healing.* Joy Degruy Publications, 2017.

Felitti, Vincent, et al. *Relationship of Childhood Abuse and Household Dysfunction to Many of the Leading Causes of Death in Adults: The Adverse Childhood Experiences (ACE) Study.* 1998.

Huber, Cheri. *There Is Nothing Wrong with You: Going Beyond Self-Hate.* Keep It Simple Books, 2001.

IPNB Workshop led by Danette C. Gillespie-Otto, LCSW, and Marc F. Otto, MA, RSMT/E, October 2019.

Levine, Peter. *In an Unspoken Voice: How the Body Releases Trauma and Restores Goodness.* North Atlantic Books, 2010.

Lonnsburry, Boni. *The Map to Abundance: The No Exceptions Guide to Money, Success, and Bliss.* The Map to Abundance, 2017.

Menakem, Resmaa. *My Grandmother's Hands: Racialized Trauma and the Pathway to Mending Our Hearts and Bodies.* Central Recovery Press, 2017.

Siegel, Daniel J. *Pocket Guide to Interpersonal Neurobiology: An Integrative Handbook of the Mind.* Norton Series on Interpersonal Neurobiology. Kindle Edition.

Walton, Adara. *Every Body's Truth Muscle Testing for the Masses.* Audver Books, 1998.

Yoder, Carolyn. *The Little Book of Trauma Healing.* Strategies for Trauma Awareness and Resilience (STAR) Resources. https://emu.edu/cjp/star/toolkit.

WELLNESS TOOL KIT

The Wellness Tool Kit is provided to assist your healing journey. Resources from the book have been compiled here to assist you in growing your healing practice. The resources have been organized through Levels 1, 2, and 3 to support your healing pathway. As you find additional supportive tools and resources, make a note of them here or in your journal.

Level 1

- Box Breathing, 51
- Pursed Lip Breathing, 51
- 4-7-8 Breathing, 51
- Alternate Nostril Breathing, 52
- Visualization, 52
- Music, 52

Level 2 and Level 3

NOTES

NOTES

NOTES

NOTES

To Write to the Author

If you wish to contact the author or would like more information about this book, please write to the author in care of Llewellyn Worldwide Ltd. and we will forward your request. Both the author and the publisher appreciate hearing from you and learning of your enjoyment of this book and how it has helped you. Llewellyn Worldwide Ltd. cannot guarantee that every letter written to the author can be answered, but all will be forwarded. Please write to:

Lisa Collins EdD
℅ Llewellyn Worldwide
2143 Wooddale Drive
Woodbury, MN 55125-2989

Please enclose a self-addressed stamped envelope for reply,
or $1.00 to cover costs. If outside the U.S.A., enclose
an international postal reply coupon.

Many of Llewellyn's authors have websites with additional information and resources. For more information, please visit our website at http://www.llewellyn.com.